MW01235722

GOD's
Miracle
Process

Trauma *Transformed* into Treasures

GOD's *Miracle* Process

Trauma *Transformed* into Treasures

Answers for Survivors of trauma and tragedy.
Supporters of Survivors
will gain inside perspectives of those you care about!

Mary J. Taylor

Mary J. Taylor is a pseudonym.
The story is true and factual, therefore, identities
have been protected by pseudonyms for anonymity.

To schedule speaking appointments
please contact the author by writing to:
Choices International
PO Box 408, Berrien Springs MI 49103
or email the author at:
yourchoices@choicesinternational.info

Cover Design by Penny Hall
Text Design by Greg Solie – Altamont Graphics

ISBN 0-9768530-0-0

CONTENTS

PREFACE

PREFACE

Why would I *choose* a life that created more problems and more trauma than when I was a child? Why would a minister's wife *choose* to divorce her husband and tell God she did not know who He is?

Why was I molested and raped as a child? How could God allow a little girl to be so violated, disrespected and abused?

Basically, I divorced my parents and siblings. They did not know of my destructive, life-altering decisions I made that Christmas day, 1994.

November 11, 1995 was a day of relief. God told me what I needed to know and **GOD's** *Miracle* **Process** was to continue in my life.

I was *not* healed from my traumas in a moment. The Holy Spirit takes us at our pace, so it is a *process*. It's a process of learning what concepts we believe that are Satan's deceptions and replacing them with Jesus' truth about ourselves and relationships (John 16:13).

November 11, 1995 my life *improved* but Satan kept working to hurt me. After I was not able to retrieve my first marriage, I married a man I met at church. It was not "until death do us part." My *choices* and experience have taught me life lessons that God never wanted His daughter to learn.

Jesus does not want evil and abuse to happen to His children (Matthew 6:13). Instead, He gave His life for us. It is Satan's *lie* that God's job is to stop bad things happening to us. God respects us and allows all of us to make *choices.* He even allows us to make *choices* that injure and damage people. God never forces us to make the right *choices.*

What is God's job? Two thousand years ago, Jesus *chose* to deliver and heal us, and to give us insight and wisdom for all our situations. Jesus came to show and tell the Good News of His love and His value for each *victim and survivor* in the midst of our pain and trauma (Luke 4:18)! His love, respect and healing establishes our *self-value!*

In this book, S*upporters* can see what we think, how we feel, what we need and what S*upporters* can do that is helpful and productive for us in our pain. Do *you* care enough about people who seem to keep having serious problems, to take time to learn what you can do that helps them?

Read slowly and think seriously about this information. No doubt God wants to use *you* in **GOD's *Miracle* Process** in the lives of some of *your* family and friends.

The purpose of this book is not to reveal what people have done to me. *My purpose is to reveal Satan's deceptions and attempts to destroy us, and to reveal Jesus' great love for each of us and His healing process.*

I love my parents (Dad is resting in Jesus), my siblings and each extended family member. No attitude or action is worth more than having a relationship with God and my family. I thank God for each of my friends. *Thank you to each person who has believed in me and supported me through* **GOD's** *Miracle* **Process**.

May each sister and brother in Jesus who reads these pages see that **GOD's** *Miracle* **Process** is available to each one of us. My prayer is that soon you, dear reader, and I will be together with our Jesus, when *He will wipe away our last tears!*

DEDICATION

DEDICATION

I dedicate this book to my Savior, Comforter and Heavenly Father. Thank you, Jesus, for *choosing* to not quit when Your life was traumatic and terrorizing for You, so You could offer me my gift of salvation. Thank you, Heavenly Father, for standing by me no matter what I *choose*. Thank you for the self-value You have established in me. Thank you, Holy Spirit, for giving me continual comfort and wisdom.

Thank you for helping me to retrieve my child faith in You. Thank you for telling me we all get to *choose,* even when our *choices* hurt other people. Thank you for *gently* leading me into Your truth and for resolution of my issues that only Your wisdom can give me. Thank you for *Your power to change* my ways of thinking.

Thank you for what my re-baptism means to me. *It feels so good to be connected to You again.* No one or no situation can take You from me now as I *choose* to stay connected to You (Romans 8:35-39). I am so happy that now I can trust You and rest every concern about my life, in Your big hands. No matter what humans *choose* to do that injures me it is a comfort knowing that You will always will be with me! Thank you for **OUR** *miracle* **process!**

QUALIFICATION TO AUTHOR

I am not a medical doctor, psychologist or therapist. I am not licensed or certified. I am God's witness (Isaiah 43:10). When the Holy Spirit comes to us He will give us power and then we will be witnesses for Jesus (Acts 1:8). *I am commissioned by God* to witness to you what I know now, and what I've seen.

I had a *private childhood* life and a *public childhood* life. My known or public life revealed a happy family with my parents, sisters and brothers. I thank each of them for the contribution they've made to my life that makes it meaningful.

I had an anxious and depressing private life. This life was full of sexual abuse, trauma, confusion and the loss of correct understanding about many issues of life and God.

My Heavenly Father was with me through all my tragedy and abuse. He has supplied insights to help me see my deceptions about Himself, myself and others. I share with you what my Heavenly Team has done for me.

My story is about God. It's about the power and wisdom of my Savior. My part is to *choose* to cooperate with God so together we can do **GOD's *Miracle* Process** for my life.

CAUTION TO READERS

S ome readers may feel uncomfortable reading the first chapter. Much more could be added to this real story but it serves the purpose. It is the story of a little girl's life. The girl grows up and faces more tragedy and trauma in her adult life because of Chapter One.

There are so many reasons why people make good and bad *choices*. Some *choices* are made out of pain and discouragement. If you read every page between these two covers you may discover some reasons why you or others you care for make the *choices* they do.

We all need to know we are valuable to our family and friends. Every one needs to see and feel love and acceptance demonstrated to them. As you read each chapter, may I suggest that you *choose* to ask God how you can specifically use this information in reaching out to *your* acquaintances, friends and family.

You will be blessed.

WHY IS THIS HAPPENING TO ME?
Chapter One

*N*o! Not again! Get out of here! I thought. I was angry again and so I shouted, *"Get out! Get out!"* My door was locked.

How did he get in here? If he can still get into my bedroom when my door is locked, I'm just not safe anywhere.

I was a little girl, only 12 years old, and anxious. I knew how girls got pregnant and I met every qualification.

Am I going to have a baby? Why is this happening to me? Brothers are not supposed to make their sisters pregnant. How will I know if I'm pregnant? Oh yeah, when I stop having my period. I'll just start getting a big tummy like my married sisters. What will people think about me? What can I do about this? I am not supposed to have a baby! What would happen to my baby?

Do my other sixth-grade girlfriends worry about having a baby? How can I look like the other girls and talk like them so they won't know anything is wrong with me?

I wanted to look normal at school and church, and act like nothing was wrong. I had a big secret and I didn't like it. My private life was embarrassing.

"Bye. We'll be back just as soon as we can." Mom and Dad were assuring me of their soon return from their business outing.

But why do they keep leaving me? I don't like the naked games I have to play when they are gone. Why is this happening to me? Is this supposed to happen to all little girls or is there something wrong with me? What did I do that makes my brother keep playing these terrifying games with me? I keep telling him I don't like it.

I don't remember when my brother, Alex, started playing these games with me. I was too young to know how old I was.

If it was not bad to play naked games Alex would play them in front of Mom. I feel like I'm bad when I have to play them. I feel sad. I feel alone. I feel angry. Mom and Dad don't play games like this with me.

"Come on and hurry up! Stand in front of the window on this stool," was my brother's order.

Alex is such an angry person. I'm afraid of what would happen to me if I don't do what he tells me I have to do when our parents are not home. I don't ever want to know what he'd do to me if I disobeyed him.

My clothes were already off my little body because we had been playing hide-and-seek naked. So it did not take me long to stand on the stool just the way I was ordered. It was dark outside and the lights were on in the house making it very easy for people to see me. There I was, exposed to the traffic as people drove past our house. I stood straight as the tree that gave me a little protection from the road.

Do people see me standing here? Oh God, please make this end. I am so ashamed. Why is this happening

14

to me? I must not be worth much or I would not have to do this. This must be my fault.

Later Mom and Dad did come home and the humiliation ended, for that night.

So often the nights brought terrifying and traumatizing dreams. In my dreams someone would be chasing me down our busy road and my little body was naked. I could never run fast enough. I would wake up feeling terrorized.

Do the kids at church and school know I'm scared? Can they tell that's happening to me?

I thought I had to pretend and act like I was a happy, contented little girl. Inside, my heart was breaking. I didn't know I could trust some people. It didn't come to my mind that some people were safe people. I didn't know I could tell some people about the terror I was living with silently inside. I didn't know that some people would have helped me, if they had known my private life.

I would wake up so afraid after dreaming that people came into my house when I knew I had tightly locked the house. Sometimes I dreamed that the locks would not work and that there was no way I could keep anyone out of my house if they wanted in.

I have no safe place. People can do anything to me. I feel so angry.

"Shhh. Be quiet, and don't slam the door or you'll wake up Mom," Alex threatened.

My family had been to church and the kitchen was cleaned up after eating dinner. Now it was time to rest. But Alex had different plans. He was taking me to his favorite place under a grove of trees in the field. It was a familiar place to me that I hated.

15

"Why are you walking so slow? Right here is good. I'll put the blanket down here and now hurry up and get your clothes off!" Alex's angry orders were frightening to my young mind. All my protesting never mattered to Alex.

I want to just run away. Alex is so much stronger than me. I can't do anything to make this nightmare stop. I hate Alex so much. I wonder why my brother hates me so much that he keeps doing this to me. I hate these secrets.

Alex knew he had power to make me do what he wanted. He used his power over me every chance he got.

"Alex it hurts! Please stop," I pleaded. Alex never stopped until he was done.

Why does He do this to me? Did someone do this to my big sisters when they were little girls? I can't tell them what Alex does to me because I'm sure I'll get into more trouble than this. I feel all alone.

"Now just do what I say and put it in your mouth!" Alex ordered.

"In my mouth? I can't. I feel sick," I protested.

"Yes, you can. Just do it, now!" was Alex's next order.

Oh God, what is happening to me? It is so big. This wet stuff in my mouth is so gross! I'm gagging. I'm going to throw up. He stinks and I feel sick.

What have I done wrong that this is happening to me? Is this my fault? What did I do to deserve my brother treating me like this?

Do people know what Alex does to me and they just don't say anything to me about it? Are they talking about me? Do they know my body hurts? Do they know

I'm afraid? Do they care that I feel so terrified when Mom and Dad are gone? Do Mom and Dad know that Alex is doing all these horrible, bad things to me?

I did not feel safe talking to anyone about the horror in my small life. It may have been safe to tell *some* people but I did not know that. I lived with my terrifying secrets alone. So of course, I felt alone.

My pain was much bigger than my small self. It took so much energy to just live through another day, and through another episode of abuse. I did not know how to help myself. Neither did I know that some people would have given *anything* to have helped me. So I lived in silence with my secrets, anxiety and anger.

My little body grew up so tense and stressed. My young mind was in a continual state of confusion. I always had to think about how to protect and defend myself from danger when possible.

You see, I did not grow up on the streets of some ugly city. I grew up in a large Christian community where Satan works hard to destroy Jesus' children. I grew up in a Christian family.

During these years of terror I certainly did not understand what was happening to me. I did not know it was called incest, sexual abuse, rape, molestation, and exhibitionism. I only knew it was wrong and that I didn't like it.

I did *not* deserve to have my life begin with such feelings, thoughts and concerns. As a child there was nothing I could do to make me responsible for what my brother did to me. I definitely was not responsible for my brother's *choices.*

Jesus did not want my brother to *choose* to do these abusive things to His little girl (Matthew 18:6). That is

17

why He was with me all the time and helped me survive these years of trauma, torture, tragedy, and pretending my private life did not exist (Matthew 28:20).

I wish I had understood this when I was a child. I didn't know that **GOD's** *Miracle* **Process** was happening for me. It was **GOD's** *Miracle* **Process** that made little Mary survive.

Why did this happen to me? Now I understand that Satan used the *choices* of my brother to set up my life for potential problems when I became an adult. Because I am Jesus' child, I understand clearly now, that Satan wants to destroy me and will torture me as much as he's allowed (John 10:10).

Eventually, I learned that God had helped me, His little lamb, survive during my abuse. And that He was going to do more to help me now. Through **GOD's** *Miracle* **Process** He would help me figure out how to have a happy, fulfilling life in spite of my brother's *choices* (John 10:10). But, that would take time.

Chapter Two

"Happy birthday, dear Mary, happy birthday to you!"

How nice for my family to sing happy birthday to me. I've waited a long time to be a teenager like my big sisters and brothers.

"Happy 13, Mary!"

Recognition made my little heart feel so good. It relieved just a tiny bit of my pain. I desperately needed all the positive comments I could get because of my private life and private pain.

My parents, siblings, and other relatives did not know how much I craved and needed their kind and supportive words. When I heard them, what a gift those words were to my lonely and abused heart! I needed more positive reinforcement than usual to help me with all my terrorizing experiences, anger, and pain.

My relatives and friends could not know *how* much their thoughtfulness and attention meant to me. They did not know the terror I was dealing with every day.

I never knew when the sexual abuse would happen again. My brother, Alex, did not know how much agony he was causing in my heart.

19

When will it happen to me again? Does Alex have enough things to do now on Sabbath afternoon so he won't make me go out to the field again? Oh God, please don't let this happen to me again. Please.

I was so afraid of what Alex would make me do every time Mom and Dad left me at home with him. He could see my body was maturing as I was getting older. He knew it was getting more and more dangerous to be penetrating his sister.

Will Alex leave me alone or not? I am so afraid he will come into my bedroom again with my door locked. I don't know how to make Alex stop. I don't think people will believe me if I tell them. So I can't get anyone to help me. When will it happen again?

In seventh grade my classmates and I had to go to a new school. I carried my anxiety with me into the hallways and classrooms of my new school.

Can my new friends tell there is something wrong with me? I don't want them to know what my other classmates probably know about my life. I just want to be normal and be like my friends.

Only time would tell me when or if the abuse would happen again.

I am so tired from always being on guard. I don't know where I'm safe, if anywhere. Will I always worry about Alex doing these terrible, hateful things to me? I'm exhausted from doing all I can to defend myself from an attack.

This daily uncertainty brought more terror to my developing mind, body, and emotions.

One Sabbath morning I woke up being touched.

Oh no. Is Alex back at this again? He hasn't done anything to me in many months. Oh God, what can I do?

A good idea came to my mind. I felt a little better because I had a plan, a plan that seemed like a good one.

I'll move just a little so the person can tell I'm waking up. Hopefully he'll stop and this will be over. I'll know for sure who's doing this to me and who I'm dealing with.

My plan worked. I slightly moved. He realized he'd better stop if he was not going to get caught. As he stood up and carefully walked toward the door I could clearly see who my abuser was this time.

It's not Alex! It's not Alex! Oh, I am so thankful. Oh, yes!

My molester was a guest in our home. I felt like I had a small amount of control with this guy.

If I tell Dad what just happened, I know he'll believe me. I know Dad will help me.

As soon as I thought Dad was awake I went downstairs. Mom was up and reading. Alone, I went into their bedroom and told my father about my early morning terror. I was correct. Dad did believe me. He was angry that our guest violated and molested his daughter.

"Mary, I'll talk to him!" Dad assured me.

Wow! This sure feels good. Dad really believes me! I can hardly wait to hear what Dad tells him!

"Dad, thank you for helping me," was all I could say. I was so relieved that Dad believed me. It became very obvious that Dad *chose* to believe me because very quickly my attacker was gone. Dad made him leave our home.

That Sabbath morning I went to church with my family. I tried to talk with my friends and act like nothing was wrong. It was hard even though I had many years of practice. My mind kept repeating what had just happened to me. There were lots of stories for my mind to repeat. There were so many sad and tragic stories.

Oh I hate feeling like this. I feel sick. I feel so angry. I hate this so much. I feel so dirty. I feel like I need to take a bath for the rest of the day. I just don't feel like I can get clean. I feel so invaded. I can hardly believe he did this to me. Why did he do it? I must be such a bad person.

I felt very confident telling Dad about what our guest did to me that morning. I was certain that Dad would believe me. I was correct.

What made me certain that Dad would believe me about our guest but not believe me about my brother? From the beginning of my life I realized the basis from which our home functioned.

One thing I knew was that Dad was happy with his boys. He was the one who spent the most time with them, teaching them. He was doing all he could to help them be Christians and good citizens.

How could Dad face the thought that one of his boys was doing all the evil to me that Alex was doing? Dad may think that Alex's *choices* were a personal disappointment of his own training abilities. Mother was a very supportive wife.

Later in my life, I discovered that I was right about my parents. As an adult, I revealed my traumatic childhood story. My parents did not believe my entire story. Certainly, I would not have been believed as a child. For some, questions linger about my life being as bad as I have said.

Eventually, I found out that other people really did not know what Alex had been doing to me. They were not talking about me. My friends had no idea. It was the fear and anxiety of Satan trying to terrorize me even more.

I learned that I have some very loving relatives and friends who wish I could have told them my story when I was a little girl. They would have helped me, but I did not know it. I feel relief and comfort knowing that many relatives and friends also feel my pain about the parts of my life that are difficult and that have hurt so bad for so long.

As an adult, I feel less stress knowing that my life matters to my family. It's encouraging to know they support me even though they may not fully understand my struggles. The lack of criticism and judgment for my decisions is a big help. Most relatives are always happy to see me and they pray for me.

When will it happen again? Jesus, what is wrong with me? Will I always have to be careful of people? Please make it stop.

Jesus did do for me all He could, considering He had to allow people to make their *choices.*

One of my teenage boyfriends, Nathan really liked me and thought that I was a good Christian young lady. He believed that God had some very important plans for my life. He didn't want to be responsible for messing up God's plans. These thoughts are what kept him from *choosing* to molest and rape me.

A few years ago Nathan told me this story. I listened in almost disbelief. I could hardly imagine that I was so close to more horror and trauma in my life.

"Thank you! Thank you so much! What a gift you gave me by not doing that to me!" was all I could say.

How thankful I am that Nathan made the right *choices* pertaining to my life. His right *choices* spared me more pain, confusion, and trauma.

I believe that God was telling my boyfriend that He had plans for my life. Jesus heard my prayers. He never wanted bad things happening to me (Matthew 6:13). Jesus did all He could to keep me safe from people who may have done more evil to me.

Some of my friends have been molested and raped by pastors, church elders, and school teachers. That could have also happened to me.

I am so thankful that I didn't have those experiences to add to the terror of what my brother did to me. I just thank Jesus that Satan did not get to cause more trauma and torture in my life through people's *choices*.

I can *choose* to see my life from Jesus' perspective or my own. My perspective can create a party, a pity party. Jesus' perspective gives me value as a woman. It gives me a thankful heart knowing He did all He could to help people make good *choices* affecting my life.

At first I went to the pity party. My party was not fun at all. I was alone.

My heart wanted to know the truth about God. I am thankful that I finally understand what God's role is in my life was, as His child. He was always with me, even when people made evil *choices* that injured me (Matthew 28:20). **GOD's *Miracle* Process** was happening.

Jesus was with me when I cried. He knew what my small, tear stained face looked like. Jesus was with me when I felt shame. He was with me when I thought these problems in my life were my fault and that I was responsible for them (Matthew 1:23).

Jesus knew what I was thinking. He saw the anxiety and trauma I lived with. He suffered pain because His little girl was suffering pain (Hebrews 4:15). I did not know yet about **GOD's** *Miracle* **Process** in my life. I did not know it was because of **GOD's** *Miracle* **Process** that I was alive and able to survive.

Jesus lived with me through my childhood losses and loneliness.

Jesus did not give His life for me or anyone else just so Satan could destroy and kill us. *Today*, Jesus wants us to have a valuable, fulfilling, and meaningful life (John 10:10).

WHY DID I THINK THIS?

Chapter Three

"Mary, you will need to ride a Greyhound bus home for Christmas. Someone at the Academy can take you to the bus depot."

"Dad, I've never ridden a Greyhound bus. Will I be safe?"

"Yes, you'll be fine. Just remember that Mother and I will be praying for you."

As a teenager, I learned some new things on my bus ride home. The depots had different magazines than we had at home.

At the bus depot I stood so that people could not easily see what I was looking at. The pictures were big and the people did not have much covering them, if anything at all.

Wow, very interesting. I like this. Why do I feel drawn to these pictures? I feel good. Why do I like them? Christians are not supposed to like pictures of people that look like this.

I knew I should not be looking at these magazines, so I was careful that no one could really see the pictures. My body felt good when I looked at the pictures. Why did I think this?

I am fat. I weigh too much. Other people probably think I'm fat too. I'm not pretty like my sisters. I don't like how I look when I see myself in the mirror. I should go on a diet but I can't. Mother would ask me why I was not eating better. I can't deal with any questions.

I'm not pretty and attractive like the girls in those magazines. If I could be thin maybe I'd be beautiful too. Why did I think this?

Why do I feel so alone? I have friends but people don't know me. They only know what I let them see about me. My life is so scary and horrible. I'm afraid that I am going to get in trouble for what my brother did to me. People would say it's my fault that Alex did those terrible things to me. Why did I think this?

I don't understand this, but if I was not a Christian I think I would be a prostitute. What? Where did that thought come from? I don't even really know what prostitutes do. But a Christian girl should not be thinking this. Why did I think this?

Two different times I stayed a few days with a Christian friend. On both visits I woke up with her touching my body. Immediately I knew her behavior was wrong, but I did not stop her.

I like how this feels. I know it's wrong but I do like it for right now. I can stop her if she tries to do anything to me that I don't like. She is not as strong as I am. I know I can control how much she does to me. Why did I think this?

I could *choose* to be embarrassed by the true stories about my previous life and not reveal to you my reality. I share them only because they are the *truth* about the *detrimental and evil effects of sexual abuse* on the victim.

27

Sexual abuse causes so much *confusion* in the mind, body, emotions, and about God. This is why I was thinking like this. The sexual innuendoes and the sexual activity prepared my brain for sexual thoughts and sexual behavior by male or female.

Even though sexual abuse is abuse, my brain was set up for sexual desire and drive that is beyond what God gave me. My *sexual desires and drives were increased* because of the sexual activity happening to my body and brain.

I am so thankful that Jesus helped me make *choices* that kept me from getting into prostitution and a homosexual lifestyle. Jesus would still have loved me if I had. But, He does not want me to suffer the pain and trauma of those *choices*.

At a very young age, I was seeing real body parts. Part of my sexual abuse was also seeing body parts on paper in the medical book at home. So, of course, my brain was also set up to look at them in a magazine. What my eyes saw made my body and mind sexually respond. So my drive and desire were increased and satisfied to some degree.

I *always* knew the sexual abuse that my brother was doing to me was *wrong*. Because I knew it was wrong, I felt bad about myself. I didn't like myself because Alex did bad things to me against my will. I was not capable of seeing myself for who I was or what I actually looked like. I was not fat. I only thought so.

I always thought of my head disconnected from my body. I was not able to see myself as one functioning unit. It was as though from a distance I watched myself live. It was part of what my brain did for me, just so I could live with my pain and experiences that could not make sense.

28

I was so sensitive about how I looked. Even when I went swimming with just my family I insisted on wearing a swim suit that had a little skirt to give me just a bit more cover. Maybe people wouldn't notice how fat I really was.

I wanted to be just as beautiful and desirable to other people as the pictures I saw in the magazines. I wanted people to want me as well as the girls in the pictures.

For some reason I was desirable to Alex. I did not know why. My brain got to the place that I thought it was good to be desired by *someone* even though I did not like the terrifying and horrible things he did to me. Yet I felt alone because of Alex.

Do you see the confusion for my brain, for my emotions, and for my body? Why did God let His little girl grow up with so many traumas? As I child, there was no way to understand these things.

I must be a little valuable to Alex or he would not be so interested in me. If I was a prostitute people would be interested in me too. Maybe I would be valuable to some people and experience some kind of love.

My mind actually translated the abuse that hurt me into some kind of love. In a *distorted* way the abuse gave me a sense of value as a person.

In reality, the abuse was torturing my mind, my emotions and my body. It was causing great depths of loneliness and confusion about God. Yet at the same time part of my brain was craving more of what made my life hurt.

In *no way* was any part of the sexual abuse a display of love or value. It was only abuse. It was only wrong. It was only evil.

Jesus created me when I was born and made me just the way He wanted me to be (Isaiah 43:1). Jesus had thoughts and plans for me. He wanted my life to be peaceful and not evil (Jeremiah 29:11). Jesus gave His life for me so we could spend forever together if I would believe Him (John 3:16).

Jesus told a parable about Satan, Jesus' enemy (John 10:1-18). Jesus described Satan as a sheep thief. Jesus said Satan has thoughts and plans for us too. Satan wants to kill and destroy Jesus' sheep (John 10:10). You and I are Jesus' sheep and are in need of **GOD's *Miracle* Process**.

It was Satan's plan that the sexual abuse would destroy and kill this little sheep of Jesus. I was a child who loved Jesus. Satan was working through the *choices* of my brother to devour Jesus' child (I Peter 5:8).

As a teenager and an adult, Satan wanted me to think the effects of the sexual abuse were good for me. Instead of love and value for me, it was an opportunity Satan used to confuse my mind and emotions.

All the confusion in my body, emotions and brain was the enemy's plan to keep me from understanding God's love and value for me. My family always loved me and valued me very much. My painful, private life distorted these truths for me. **GOD's *Miracle* Process** would help me deal with my confusion.

Satan was using Alex's *choices* as a trap for me. He wanted this trap to affect the rest of my life, however long that might be. Maybe I would even *choose* to shorten my life because of the depressing pain. Satan could wish. Yes, I had great need of **GOD's *Miracle* Process**.

God had plans to help me overcome all my terrorizing dreams, confusion, pain, hate and anger, resulting from my brother's *choices*. I thank Jesus so much that His power is greater than Satan's influence in my life (I John 4:4).

DO I HAVE TO TELL?
Chapter Four

"Tell him what happened to you." The thought seemed almost loud enough to hear. "What? I'm not telling him," I protested.

Again the thought came to me, "Tell him!"

"But I can't tell him. Do I have to tell?" I questioned.

Again the thought was very clear, "Tell him!"

"Okay, I will."

I was sitting on my couch as I finished my personal time with God that morning. I did not understand why I should tell. I did not want to tell.

My boyfriend, Joel and I decided we wanted to get married. This morning I was told to tell Joel about what my brother, Alex, did to me when I was a little girl.

Oh no, I sure don't want to go there. What's it got to do with Joel? He doesn't need to know.

When we went for our morning walk I was not quite so bubbly. My thoughts were disturbing to me. I was quiet. I was thinking.

I love Joel and I do not know why I should tell him about the black, painful part of my life. Alex has not done anything bad to me for ten years so why bring this up? Do I have to tell? I really don't like thinking about Alex.

God gave me courage. "Honey, I need to tell you a story."

"Okay."

But I didn't know how to tell the story. Finally, these words came out of my mouth. "I need to tell you when I was growing up I had sex with my brother. I don't do it anymore. It ended many years ago."

Glad I got that over with. I did what I had to do. I've never told anyone before.

"What? Mary, you did what?"

Joel was angry. Joel was angry with me for being so stupid.

How are we ever going to work through this? See, I knew I should not have told him. God, I told Joel because I heard you tell me to tell him. Now what am I supposed to do?

Joel had a story to tell me. That same morning he asked God to show him anything else he needed to know about me before we got married. These two stories were interesting when we put them together. Joel asked for a story and God told me what story to tell him.

"Do I have to tell?" was my question because of my unusual instructions.

Years later, I found many answers to this question. God was helping me even though it did not look like it that morning. God brought Joel from one part of the country and me from another and we met in New England. God knew that Joel would love me even though I could not change the disgusting parts of my childhood.

God provided Joel to help me as my husband (Isaiah 43:4). God knew the best time for Joel to learn the truth about me so he could help me during our marriage. Would he have wondered what else I was hiding from him if I told him my "secrets" after we were married?

Doing what God told me to do that morning, God was working to create a safe place for me in Joel's heart (Proverbs 1:33). It was necessary for Joel to understand more about my life experiences, because later, together God would help us deal with my confusion, pain, anger and terror.

God was with me and helping me survive what Alex did to me during my young years. God did all He could to help people make *choices* that would not hurt me. Now, God was providing a husband for me who would make *good choices*.

Even from the beginning of my traumatic and abusive life, I was valuable and precious to Jesus. He loved me. God knew of people who would make efforts to understand me so I could eventually be free of my torture and agony (Isaiah 43:4). God had thoughts, plans, and desires for me to learn how to have a peaceful, contented life (Jeremiah 29:11).

God's assistance in my life is what I call **GOD's *Miracle* Process.** God thought Joel would be a valuable part of **GOD's *Miracle* Process** for me. God saw He could use Joel to help transform my traumas into God's treasures.

"Do I have to tell?" was my question. The answer had to be, "Yes," so God could use my husband to help me!

Chapter Five

"**M**ary, you said you did what?"

"I said when I was growing up I had sex with my brother, and that we don't do it anymore. We stopped many years ago." I felt terrible telling him this story.

My husband-to-be, Joel, was so angry that I would be so stupid to have sex with my brother, Alex, when I was a child.

Yeah, it was stupid to me, too. I hated it. There was nothing I could do to make it stop. I wanted it to stop. It hurt and it still does. I feel like such a fool. I feel so stupid to have had sex with my brother.

Joel loved me and we got married a few weeks later. We tried to forget my story about Alex. It only brought stress to our marriage. There was never much to discuss about it because a brother and sister having sex is so ridiculous. Until one day.

I walked up to my husband with the newspaper in my hand, "Honey, look at what I just read. This is an interesting story. I have a name." My husband stood there in the kitchen just looking at me wondering what I meant.

"Of course you have a name. I like your name."

"My name is Victim. I am a victim of sexual abuse. That is what happened to me. I did not have sex with

35

my brother. That was sexual abuse. Alex molested me. Alex raped me. That is called incest." Joel just looked at me and he got angry again.

This time Joel was not angry with me. He was angry with my brother. How dare Alex do such things to his wife?

"Oh, Honey, I love you. I'm sorry. It's not your fault. I am so sorry."

I'm so thankful Joel's not angry with me about this now. I'm glad someone else is angry with Alex. This feels good. What relief. Joel said it was not my fault. I always thought there was something I did wrong that caused my problems.

Why did I tell Joel that I had sex with my brother? Because I thought I did. That is one reason why I thought I was bad. That is why I felt shame. That is why I felt responsible. My body responded sexually to some of the things Alex did to me. My body functions made me think I wanted what he did to me even though it hurt, and I hated Alex for doing it all.

Why did I tell Joel that I had sex with my brother? I had never put in words what Alex did to me. Joel was the first person that I told my story to. I got it all wrong.

Why did I change my story? Was I lying? Or did I not understand? I understood nothing about what Alex had done to me for so many years, except that I hated it and that it was wrong. I did not know that I was a victim of sexual abuse and incest.

Finally, I realized the difference. I was relieved to know I never had sex with my brother. Instead, my brother penetrated me. Because it was a relative that sexually abused me, my abuse was also called incest.

I remember reading that one out of five girls would be sexually molested by age eighteen. And one out of ten boys would be sexually molested by age eighteen. No one asked me, so more people are molested than what these numbers reveal.

Wow, I feel better knowing that so many people know how I feel. They know how devastated and dirty I feel. They understand why I feel so angry and abandoned.

The newspaper story taught me that thoughts about prostitution were a result of my sexual abuse. The girl in the story had so many problems because of her life as a victim of sexual abuse and now as a prostitute.

I am so thankful to finally know why those thoughts about being a prostitute have been in my head. What a relief to understand that I am normal about those confusing thoughts, even though it's disgusting. It was just a result of the abuse. This story helps me see that I have been saved from an even more terrifying life since I did not get involved in prostitution.

Learning the truth about my trauma, sexual abuse, and incest gave Joel and me the truth to deal with. This information was another part of **GOD's** *Miracle* **Process** for me. Knowing that I did not cause the abuse and that I was not responsible for the abuse helped us proceed in my healing and recovery process. This truth about myself helped me feel free (John 8:32).

This correct understanding made life better but our lives were not easy. Situations came up we didn't want to deal with, yet we had strength and did not quit (Isaiah 41:10). Sometimes our lives were stressful and very tough, but we found that God gave us what we needed (Isaiah 40:29, 31). We were in the middle of **GOD's** *Miracle* **Process** for my healing.

37

HAPPY, HAPPIER, OR HAPPIEST?

Chapter Six

"**J**oel, I'm almost ready. I've been looking forward to our visit. These two have almost become family to us." My husband and I were on our way to see guests of our church.

The two of us were so happy that God brought our lives together. Joel and I were full of energy and looking forward to what life would bring for us together. Our desire was for God to use our lives to help people.

Joel was a pastor, which meant I was a pastor's wife. I worked with Joel on church projects and supported him administratively. We visited members and guests of our church. Joel and I loved working together. We were an effective team. Our hearts seemed to beat together!

We were happy when Joel's boss told him that he was going to be ordained as a minister. Joel's ordination was a highlight for us.

My husband loved adventure. My life growing up was mostly serious. I used so much energy on just surviving that I didn't have much left for doing new things just for fun. I liked adventure but it required so much energy.

Joel's adventurous personality was good. It was part of **GOD's** *Miracle* **Process** for me. Things we did gave a freshness and newness to my life that God knew I needed in my process.

Our honeymoon was great. "Honey, hurry and get up! Look out the window. I'm going outside to take pictures." I got up quickly wondering what Joel was talking about.

What is that bear doing? Amazing. He's standing on his hind legs helping himself to what's in that car. He's got a head of lettuce. He just tossed it away. He doesn't like lettuce. Now he has peanut butter. Look at that. He's so smart.

He laid the jar on the ground with his paw on it. With his other front paw he just popped the lid off. He really liked the peanut butter.

We saw "Sugar Bear" in other places during our stay at Sequoia National Park in California. He was a wild friend in the park who had learned to find and enjoy campers' food. It was great fun, until the day we got ready to go home.

"Honey, look at this!" As I called to Joel, I could hardly believe what I saw. Sugar Bear had been to visit us. He left his signature twice on the driver's door just below the window. His front paw prints were very distinct. We were especially thankful that we did not leave food in the car since my parents loaned us their van!

Every few weeks Joel and I attended some kind of cultural event. I never went to professional musical concerts and symphonies when I was growing up. I discovered my favorite place to sit was where I could see the orchestra play their various instruments. Eating at our favorite restaurants was part of the experience.

"Mary, how about going spelunking?" Joel questioned.

I don't have energy for that. I don't want to do that. I feel tired.

"You will need to sign this before we go," our guide told us.

"What's this?" I was almost convinced it might be fun to go spelunking. This waiver released the cave management of any fault in case we were injured or killed on our cave adventure. I tried to be a good sport.

Joel and I put on our knee pads and a helmet with a light on the front of it. I was thankful for my flashlight. I'd never crawled on my tummy before in a cave. But it was worth it, if I was going to get out! We did see some beautiful parts of nature that were new to me.

After feeling brave that I really *chose* to go spelunking, Joel got another bright idea. "Since we live in New England now, we really ought to learn how to downhill snow ski."

H-m-m-m, I didn't know it was mandatory to downhill ski to live in New England. I guess my husband thinks so. I don't think I want to do that. It will take far too much energy. I'm too tired.

"Is the bunny trail open this morning?" my husband was on the phone talking with someone at the ski resort. Friends were visiting us for a few days and so the four of us decided to learn to ski together. The bunny trail was challenging enough for me.

All of us were looking forward to our lessons the next day. We got up early and drove an hour to get to the ski resort. "Our beginner slope is not open today. It doesn't have enough snow on it. It's too icy." We didn't know slopes close due to ice and not enough snow cover from day to day.

We were at the resort. What should we do? We *chose* to do intermediate lessons. The four of us rode the lift to the top of the slope. Our instructor did her best to give instruction and courage. I did receive her instruction but not her courage. I was scared beyond words.

The hill not only looked like a mountain that went straight down but it was an icy mountain that went straight down. In order for me to get to the bottom of the hill I mostly went on my bottom side! That was not fun but I *tried* to be a good sport.

Eventually, I did learn the fun and joy of downhill skiing. It was good exercise in the fresh air. The sights of nature were spectacular. Joel's adventurous personality was good for me once again. I was happy to learn a new sport.

Thanksgiving was Joel's favorite holiday and Christmas was mine. In our home we made both days special. Decorating for the holidays was one of my specialties and worth the energy it took.

We bought houses as necessary to meet our needs and work assignments. I loved decorating and playing with our houses. It was creative and relaxing for me.

"Joel, I wish I had gone to college when I finished high school. But, I'm not smart enough to go to college. There is no point in thinking about it." Joel could not understand why I said that.

"Honey, you are smart. You would get good grades and it would be a good experience for you."

"But Joel, how do you know I'd get good grades?" I was surprised that he thought I was smart.

"I see how you work hard on projects. I see how you think."

With Joel's encouragement and belief in me, I enrolled in our local community college. *I did not know that God made me intelligent like other people. This really feels good. I have chosen to study and do my assignments, but I am totally amazed to be doing so well. This is really worth the energy.*

I had been so affected by the abuse that I didn't know my value. I thought I was rather stupid. What a fabulous adventure realizing the truth about the way God made me.

God and I were slowly doing a process together showing me who Mary really was. He had a lot to teach me about myself. **GOD's *Miracle* Process** taught me a little at a time as I could understand it and make it part of what I believed about who I am (John 16:13). God's wisdom and truth about myself was making me so much happier (Proverbs 3:13).

My life with Joel is so valuable. He is so supportive of the reasons for my pain and trauma. It comforts me to know the incest and abuse makes Joel angry too. I love Joel so much for the respect and care he has for me.

Joel and I found great pleasure in doing things together, work or play. We were in love and appreciated each other for who we were. We definitely planned to grow old together. Joel's adventurous personality was so good for my healing process. Joel's adventures were part of **GOD's *Miracle* Process** for me. God wanted me to be happy, and even happier than ever.

WHY IS IT SO HARD TO DO?
Chapter Seven

"I can't. It hurts. Honey, please be patient with me. I'm sorry."

My husband and I were just doing what God made our bodies to do. Joel and I were physically attracted to each other. We were sexually motivated.

This is strange. We've been married a few years by now and it keeps getting harder for me to make love. What in the world is wrong with me?

Sometimes during our lovemaking my incest experiences came to my mind.

This smells so disgusting. I think I'm going to throw up. My throat feels like its closing. It is so big. Why did my brother do that to me? Alex, I hate you for doing this to me. I remember that field. I felt terrible, and it hurt.

You not only ruined my life as a child but you're ruining it now, too. Just get out of my life, Alex, and don't ever come back. I don't care what happens to you. The sooner you die the better.

There was no way my body could function properly with these thoughts and feelings. My husband was lying there with me trying to be patient. He was waiting for me. I'd cry knowing that anything that felt good was not going to happen for me now, or for Joel.

My muscles tightened and constricted. My nerve endings had no good sensations. My nerves were dealing with fear, trauma, hate and repulsion. I could not enjoy the sexual function that God made my body to enjoy.

It was *another* disappointing lovemaking experience for both of us. Joel and I were angry about what was happening to me. My problems affected Joel. That was really unfair and that made me angry too.

This is so unfair to Joel. It breaks my heart to see Joel suffer because of my incest. It's wrong. If only Alex knew what he's doing to us.

After so many devastating months I realized that I had to do something to get control over my mind and body.

There must be something I can do about this. Oh God, you know the problems I have. You know what this is doing to Joel. I hate this happening to Joel. It is not his fault.

I was determined to take control of myself. I must be in charge of what happened to me now.

I am angry that now, when I am supposed to enjoy sex and lovemaking that I am having a hard time. When I was not supposed to, I was forced. Alex controlled my life as a child, and he is still controlling my life. That really makes me furious.

I decided my situation was mind over matter. I must *choose* how I will think.

This is my husband. He loves me. Joel will not hurt me. He will not force me. God made me to enjoy this, so I will. Everything is alright. I am Okay. God will help me do whatever I need to do to correct my sexual problems (Philippians 4:13).

44

As I asked God to help me know how to change my responses and thoughts I found God's solution (James 1:5). God helped me focus and control my mind when the disgusting thoughts and feelings came to me (Romans 12:2).

Keeping my mind focused on what God was helping me with also gave me peace when Alex came to my mind (Isaiah 26:3). **GOD's** *Miracle* **Process** was to help me with all aspects of my life. My body began functioning properly as I practiced the discipline of what I thought about. In time, this did resolve our sexual problems.

Obviously this was *our* problem. In a sense, my husband was a victim of sexual assault also. That was so wrong and devastating to our marriage. God continued to give us the help we needed to go on.

The longer we were married the harder Satan worked to mess up the good thing God created our marriage to accomplish. God made our marriage to assist with **GOD's** *Miracle* **Process** for me and for me to give to Joel.

Satan was using my marriage to hurt me. He was trying to keep the past in our marriage. The enemy was working for my childhood to traumatize all of my life, always (I Peter 5:8). I discovered that Jesus' power to help me overcome and be in control is much greater than Satan's power to make me miserable and unable to function (I John 4:4).

A BABY FOR MARY?

Chapter Eight

"We've prayed about it and it seems to me that God wants us to have a baby in our family." My husband and I had been discussing and praying about a baby. Should we have a baby? Does God think we should have children?

"Honey, I agree. When do you think we should start trying to have our baby?" I wanted Joel to say, "Right now!" I wanted to be pregnant. I wanted a baby and to be a mother. So this conversation was very good news.

We've been married five years. I know it's good that we didn't have a child before now. This is so exciting. I can hardly wait. I'm 28 years old. This is a good time for me to have a baby. I feel so good about this. Yes, the time has come!

I started looking at baby things in the stores and dreaming. I bought a book so we could find the best name for our baby. It was so much fun to anticipate a baby in our home. I knew something of what it might be like because of all my nephews and nieces I grew up around. I loved babies. I loved children.

I also knew a piece of reality. Not every couple gets pregnant right away, unfortunately. So we began our baby pursuit knowing it might take time. We were patient. Three years later Joel and I decided it was time for me to be a patient!

I tried to find a good fertility doctor. I needed a doctor who would seriously determine what the issues were. *We* wanted a baby. Joel and I went in for tests and Joel tested perfect! I tested imperfect! I had endometriosis.

I've had two surgeries and the doctor still doesn't know why I'm not pregnant. Oh God, will I ever be able to have a baby? When I was 12 years old I was so anxious and distressed about having a baby. Now I'm 30 something and I'm anxious about having a baby. What's wrong with my life?

My desire to have a baby and all my charming dreams had faded into a mere hope. A name for our baby no longer had its appeal. This was another source of pain. Do I ever get to have control over what happens to me?

Many women came into the doctor's office where I worked telling their pregnancy stories. They tried a few months and thought they'd never get pregnant, but did. The first time some couples tried it was all done.

Why not me too? It's my turn, isn't it? Joel and I really want a baby.

No one meant to make me feel bad with their stories.

Why can't I have a baby? I can't stand to listen to these stories anymore. It hurts too much. I must have had something wrong with me growing up, or my brother would have never terrorized me like he did. Now there's something else wrong with me. Why do I have these problems? Other people don't have such a hard time, do they?

Eventually, when ladies came to work and told their stories I began making myself busy in another room. It helped a little. One day I had a bright idea. I sure needed **GOD's *Miracle* Process** to help me with this issue.

If I'm going to be unhappy about other people's happiness, I will be a very miserable person. No one will want to be my friend. This does not work for me. This is a bad way to handle life. My pity party is rather lonely.

Joel and I talked about our loss. It was heart-wrenching for both of us. We really wanted to be parents. We discussed therapies, supplements, and adoption. Finally, we decided to leave our situation in God's hands. If I got pregnant fine, if not, we'd just accept it.

One day I heard that maybe the reason I did not get pregnant had to do with my sexual abuse. That is not good news.

My body had to deal with large amounts of stress while it was developing. My muscles were usually tight and constricted. Of course, my body cannot properly function now. It never has.

This thought made me angry again at Alex. What cruelty to cause so many problems in my life.

What did he think he was doing? Was it some kind of game or power trip? It's not a game for me. You've ruined my life, Alex. Oh, I hate you.

My brother took my innocent childhood from me. Now Alex has taken from me my ability to give a childhood to my own child. What a big price for a little girl and a woman to pay!

Joel and I knew God understood our disappointment, loss, and grief about us not having our own children

(Isaiah 53:4). Our fertility situation hurt, but we knew God was helping us deal with it because we were in **GOD's** *Miracle* **Process** (II Corinthians 12:9).

(Isaiah 53:4). Our fertility situation hurt, but we knew
God was helping us deal with it because we were in
GOD's Miracle Process (II Corinthians 12:9).

DO I HAVE TO GO THROUGH IT AGAIN?

Chapter Nine

"You don't know what you're talking about.
Just shut up and listen to me." I was angry
with my husband.

*God, I am so tired of fighting and arguing with
Joel. I get angry with him over the smallest things.
Why do I do that? It seems like I'm always angry
about something.*

"Joel, I'm sorry. I shouldn't talk to you like that. I
get so frustrated and angry. I just realized it's really not
you I'm angry with. I'm just taking my anger out on
you. Honey, I am so sorry."

If I wasn't angry with Joel then who was I
angry with?

The trauma from the incest and sexual abuse that
my brother, Alex, caused me as a child was not enough
trauma for the enemy. Satan wanted to create as much
damage to my life as possible. The first round of abuse
was not enough for the enemy, so as an adult he was
going for his second round with me. Do I have to go
through it again?

*Satan is using my childhood torture and abuse as
his basis for my trauma and tragedies now as an adult.
This makes me so angry with him. I hate my brother
and the devil.*

Joel and I had been married eight years when thoughts about my incest started coming to my mind more often. I didn't like thinking about Alex and the pain he brought me. Joel and I were happy even though I got angry with him. He really did know I was sorry. Our lives together meant a lot to us.

The more I thought about the sexual abuse that I survived, the more I became unhappy.

Why did this happen to me? I absolutely did not deserve to be treated like that. I can't even enjoy the pleasure of lovemaking like I should because of it. Now I don't have a baby either. I'm so angry with Joel. This is all so wrong. This is not fair.

I began reading and talking with a few people about sexual abuse and how families function or don't function. My unhappiness increased. Injustices in my life became more obvious to me. I tried to be a nice person but my anger from childhood was becoming more familiar to Joel.

If I could find a good Christian therapist or counselor I think it would help me. I would understand my life better. Joel and I would be happier again. I want to be a good person. I want to be happy like a Christian should be.

I called many counseling offices trying to find a Christian woman that I thought I might be able to trust some of my life with. I'd never asked anyone like this to help me before. It was all new to me and I was a little nervous about it.

I must go with an open mind if I'm going to get any help and learn what I need to know. I am only going twice a month. That's enough.

51

The more I did my counseling and therapy, the more I read, the more I talked about my childhood, the more absorbed I became with myself. I was focusing on myself and what I liked and didn't like. I found out I didn't like some of Joel's attitudes either.

If I can only understand what I need to know then I can get these tragedies and abuse behind me. I want to know how to get rid of this pain that is just excruciating. Can our friends tell that I'm a survivor of sexual abuse? I don't want them to know. Our friends mean a lot to me and I don't want that to change.

As my counseling and therapy caused me to focus more on myself, I began wondering what people meant by things they said. I began questioning people's motives. I began trusting people less than before. I became more suspicious of people.

Is my life getting better or worse? I guess my life is sort of supposed to get worse before it can get better. Kind of like, "No pain, no cure." I certainly know what pain is. In time, I think Joel and I will understand better what we need to do.

My relationship with my husband was not what it had been. I questioned relationships with my family. Some things about my friends and work associates bothered me more now. I thought more negatively than ever before. I was in great need of **GOD's *Miracle* Process** to get help with relationships.

"Do I have to go through it again?" was my question. Yes, because Satan is cruel. When I was a child he used Alex's *choices* to set up my life for disaster. The sexual abuse caused me anger and many things I did not correctly understand about my life and relationships.

Satan used the abuse as a basis to set me up for many adult problems. I was convinced that I needed to read and get counseling. Satan used my reading and counseling to confuse me even more. Talking about my abuse with those who did not teach me God's method of healing only created many new problems for me.

"Do I have to go through it again?" Yes, because Satan wanted to use my incest to continually make my life a problem. He was being too successful. While Alex was controlling and terrorizing my life, the devil whispered his lies in my mind. Even though Alex stopped molesting me, Satan did not stop lying to me.

"You should be so ashamed of yourself."

"You can't do anything right."

"People think you're really stupid."

"If people knew what all you've done, they would not like you."

"You are ugly and pathetic."

"You'll never be worth anything."

"People don't believe anything you say."

Satan understood the damage of these lies in my mind as a little girl. The devil knows the destruction of these lies, if I believe what he tells me (John 10:10). God does not want me to think that the enemy's lies are true about His daughter (John 8:44).

Jesus was with me during my first round and was staying with me for my second round with the enemy. Satan set a trap for me as a child that would require **GOD's *Miracle* Process** to get His adult daughter out of (I John 3:1). The devil thought he had me in a black hole and that I would never be able to get out (Psalm 40:1, 2). He would find out he was wrong!

53

Jesus wanted me to conquer the devil's attacks in my life (Romans 8:37). Jesus was going to help me understand what I needed to know and bring value and happiness to my life again (John 10:10).

WHERE CAN WE LEARN?

Chapter Ten

"It would be so much fun to scuba dive. We could go on dive vacations. What do you think?" This was at least the fourth time my husband said this to me in the last year. Joel was used to hearing me say, "If you want to dive, help yourself. I'm not interested." This time my mind raced as I remained silent for a moment.

Joel wants to scuba dive. The abuse stuff has been so hard to deal with. I've learned a lot and worked hard to change things in me. I think I can do absolutely anything now! I could learn to overcome my fear of water too. I'm sure I could learn if wanted to! Do I want to scuba dive? It will take so much energy.

"Where can we learn?" Joel could hardly believe his ears. The next day we were at the dive shop arranging our private lessons and purchasing the equipment and gear we needed.

Joel and I diligently studied our dive book and passed our written exams. The techniques we learned in the book we had to actually perform in the water before we could be certified. Our instructor, Ken had a pool in his backyard.

Ken explained the skills we were going to work on and Joel would do it first.

"I'll do it, please just give me the time I need." I could not be rushed. When I was growing up some relatives thought it was funny to scare me by holding me under the water. I could not be forced now, if my mind had to function.

Joel is here. He will not let anything happen to me. Ken is a doctor so he will know what to do to help me if I get into trouble. I am safe. I'm Okay. If other people can do this, I can too.

Ken patiently waited for me on the bottom of the pool on the deep end. I had to perform my skills in front of him. In the water I could not control exactly where my body was. That was scary because I was afraid I would literally end up on top of my instructor.

Now I had to deal with my fears of the water and the abuse, which made my learning too stressful. I had to think back to when I controlled my thoughts in bed with my husband, when Alex came to my mind (Romans 12:2). I knew God and I could do it again. I would have to discipline myself as to what I thought about.

Ken reminded me so much of my brother. The trauma that Alex created made me so afraid of ending up lying on Ken. It was beyond any idea of embarrassment. Now my sexual abuse was in my face again.

No way, Alex still has so much control of my life. I'm all anxious again trying to do what I want to do. What does incest have to do with learning to scuba dive? It was not Ken's fault. Satan never wanted to give me a break.

I have already learned how to make love when thoughts of Alex come to my mind. Certainly I can learn to scuba dive when I think of Alex.

Again I had to focus and concentrate on what I was doing. I had to control what I thought about.

Take a big deep breath. I'll remove my mask. I'll clear the water in my mask just like I learned to do. Okay. I'm ready. I'll just go slow and do for Ken what I've learned how to do.

I did it. I did well and my husband and instructor were very pleased and happy with me. They were even proud of me. I was not Ken's first student that had great fear of water. Was I his first student to deal with sexual abuse too? I didn't ask.

To be a certified scuba diver I had to swim a certain distance without touching the bottom or ends of the pool. I was already exhausted from practicing my skills. Ken made up his mind I was going to swim my laps, tired or not. My begging and feeling already wiped out did no good to convince him otherwise.

I'm not a good swimmer. I'm tired. Having to deal with the abuse here just really makes me angry. I'll never pass today. I don't want to do this, but I am determined to be a certified scuba diver, therefore I have to be determined to swim my laps. I'd better get at it.

Ken's words were encouraging. After I swam "umpteen" laps Ken cheered me on. "Keep at it; you're doing great, Mary. Only three more laps."

"Where can we learn?" turned out to be a good question. Five days after Joel and I were certified, we were in Grand Cayman doing what had been so hard for me to learn.

"Joel, it almost blows my mind that I was able to do that 90 foot deep dive with you. I can hardly believe that I am a scuba diver! It was certainly worth the effort of learning to dive!"

I spent so much energy talking to myself and talking to God so I could overcome my fears of water and sexual abuse trauma. Really, I never thought about how much fun diving would be. The fish were just beautiful. The coral, which are living animals, have such different shapes, colors, and designs.

In the water these wild animals are not so likely to move away from me like they do on land. I love animals, so being with them like this in the water was my special gift. I even got to pet stingrays in the Caribbean Sea.

"Where can we learn?" really turned out to be a good question.

Four months later Joel and I went scuba diving on Bonaire, Antilles Netherlands. It is an island just north of Venezuela where most people do not dive. So everything was pristine and unharmed in the ocean.

I look at the sea and I know what to do so I can safely enjoy the fish and coral below the surface. What a feeling of accomplishment, control, and power over my own life. God really has helped me overcome many thoughts, feelings and fears. He has helped me better understand many things about life.

I found a special underwater picture. I think of how blessed I am to enjoy my life and the life of the animals under the surface of the water. Most people are too afraid to do what it takes to enjoy these pleasures.

The picture hangs on my wall reminding me of issues God and I have overcome that had been controlling my life. I like to look at the picture and remember the discipline, the healing, and my dependence on God. It reminds me that with God I can conquer the trauma of the enemy (Romans 8:37).

"Where can we learn?" really turned out to be a good question.

"Let's go diving in the Red Sea." Did I mention that Joel was adventurous?

We took a dive cruise boat for ten days 300 miles down the Red Sea. There were nine divers and eight crew members. It didn't take long for the attentive service to spoil us.

It was spawning season in the Red Sea. We swam through schools of baby fish that were all sizes, shapes, and colors. Some of the soft coral in the Red Sea look like huge broccoli and cauliflower. The beauty is beyond my ability to describe.

Joel and I toured Egypt for a week before our dive cruise. Being in a 4,000-year-old country was hard to connect with. Cairo's old, mammoth open-air shopping bazaar was a neat adventure. We went into the Grand Pyramid and some of the tombs of the kings. We drove through the hot Sinai Desert. We saw the Sinai Mountains.

Our scuba diving adventures were good for us. It gave us needed and helpful variety. Joel and I were tired from the hard work we were doing to have a meaningful marriage.

Satan was very effective with keeping me stressed out from all the sexual abuse lies and trauma he had in my mind. Because I did not use God's help as much as I needed it, the enemy kept beating me up with his lies.

I did not keep taking God seriously enough about taking me out the black hole the devil's lies and Alex's *choices* created for me (Psalm 40:1, 2). Trusting God enough to cooperate with Him is what I have to *choose*

59

to do everyday (Joshua 24:15). I have to *choose* God's help every day because Satan lies to me every day.

My life felt like a roller coaster ride that never shut off. The scuba diving was part of **GOD's** *Miracle* **Process** for me. It was more of God's thoughts and plans for me to have peace and minimize the evil in my life (Jeremiah 29:11). Joel and I had a new common interest to share together. Our diving gave us some relief just as God planned.

WILL THEY BELIEVE ME?

Chapter Eleven

"**I**t's hard for me to believe all the things our brother did to me. So I'm sure it's hard for you to believe it, too." My sister did have a hard time thinking that our brother was a sexual abuser because she also loved Alex.

My family was getting together and I didn't want to see him.

I hate Alex. I always have to pretend I love him like my other brothers. I can't pretend anymore. This is not right. My family should know that I'm suffering. I think they would care. I think they would help me.

The more books I read and the more counseling I did, the harder it got for me to carry my secret about Alex. Now I needed the support of my family.

If they didn't know, I need to hear them tell me they did not know what Alex did to me. I want them to tell me I did not deserve this abuse. It would feel so good to hear my parents and siblings say they believe me.

My husband thought my family should know about the terror of my secret, silent life. "There is no reason for them to not know. For your sake, Honey, I wish you would tell them."

"Thank you, Joel for loving me. Thank you so much for believing me. Will *they* believe me?"

Why should I have to pretend about my life? I should be able to be who I am and admit that I hate my brother. If I can't be real with my family who can I be real with? Even my family only knows the public part of my life. I don't think they know I have this secret, private life.

I loved each of my other brothers and my sisters. I loved Mom and Dad. Because of another family reunion I needed them to know the trauma that I was dealing with. I wanted them to know the reunion was a huge stress on my life that I was not sure how to deal with, one more time.

Since Joel was not going to the reunion with me, I wanted *my family* to protect me from Alex. I needed them to make sure I didn't get stuck in some frightening or uncomfortable situation. I didn't want to feel abandoned and left to protect myself, alone again.

I am a big girl, yeah, almost 40 years old, and I want to be cared for the way I should have been cared for when I was a little girl. It would feel so good to finally have the protection of my family.

Dad and Mom took my childhood story the hardest. It was difficult for them to hear. Their daughter was traumatized and terrorized by the evil *choices* of their son. I'm sorry it was so hard for Dad and Mom.

Breaking my lifetime of silence was part of **GOD's** *Miracle* **Process** for me. By the time I shared my secret life with my family, I knew that I was *not* responsible for the incest. This helped me put our conversations into better perspective.

"Will they believe me?" was my question. Maybe they will. Maybe they won't.

I so much appreciate the support my siblings did give me. They did believe me. Many times they talked long hours with each other about what they could do for me. My siblings would have done well to have had stock in the telephone company!

Some of them even talked with Alex about making things right with me. They told him that restitution to his victim is a Bible principle, and that it is not optional.

Wow, I can hardly believe they said that to him. That's what I told Alex too. This sure makes me feel good. They really are standing up for me.

My siblings did not know how to help me. They did the best they could. They had never dealt with sexual abuse and incest before. None of us knew what to do. We all did the best we could. I appreciate each one of them for all they did.

"Will they believe me?" was my question. Yes, they believed me. They cared about my abuse and tragedies. Their concern and intervention at the time was exactly what I needed. My brothers and sisters were used in **GOD's** *Miracle* **Process** for me (Isaiah 43:4).

Whether anyone else believed me, at least *God believed me.* He saw all the trauma and terror. God saw me trying to make the abuse stop. He also heard me pleading with Alex to quit (Psalm 34:15). It was part of **GOD's** *Miracle* **Process** for me to move forward in my life whether or not people believed my story.

Satan had other plans than God's process for me. He would do all he could to interrupt it. I began needing and wanting more from my family.

YOU MEAN IT'S NOT TRUE?
Chapter Twelve

*Y*ou mean it's not true? Are you serious? How can it not be true?" I asked myself. All I ever wanted to know was the truth. I just wanted help. How can it not be true?

God had lots of things He wanted me to understand as I continued with **GOD's *Miracle* Process** in my life. God wanted me to find His relief from my pain and nightmares (Luke 4:18). How long would it take me to learn what God wanted to teach me? It would depend on how much I allowed God to lead me. I wanted help, but I was afraid.

I know I need help but I'm scared to get help. What will a counselor make me do? I'll try to not think about what Alex did to me and maybe it will all go away. But, will it ever go away?

I had problems because my brother molested me and traumatized me. Off and on I looked for a Christian counselor and therapist to help me. I thought that if a therapist was a Christian, then I would get *Christian* help. I also spent time reading books and articles about therapy written by Christians.

I really do need to be careful that I am a good example because I'm a minister's wife. I must not make any needless mistakes.

Every other week I visited my Christian counselor and therapist with an open and receptive mind. She was a woman who seemed to care. We never prayed during my visits. We never asked God to give us wisdom. She never opened the Bible or referred to the Bible in my sessions. I decided Christian counselors must not do that and that therapists and counselors knew what to do. So, I trusted her.

The books I was reading and the counselors were not leading me to the Bible for God's answers and God's psychology. Because I wanted Christian help I thought what I was learning must be part of **GOD's** *Miracle* **Process** for me. Instead of **GOD's** *Miracle* **Process**, I was focusing mostly on human answers.

I've got to learn all I can so I can put my past behind me. I want to learn as fast as I can. It will be so nice when I don't think about this stuff. Oh God, please make this quick for me.

I thought I had logical reasons for my new beliefs, so my new ideas of handling what I hated in my life did not appear to be a problem. One new belief at a time, I was losing my childhood faith in Jesus and the Bible. My new ways of handling my pain and trauma were eroding my Christian principles.

Eventually, I made decisions that were *not* based on Christian principles. In time, my childhood faith in God and the Bible eroded away and disappeared.

I became more selfish. *Why don't people care that my life hurts so bad? Why don't people do what I think they should?*

I became less trusting of people. I became more cynical and skeptical. *If people are not going to help me the way I want, then I'll remove them from my life until they do, and they must think the way I want.*

I *disconnected* from people. *I feel isolated and lonely now that I see who people really are.*

I believed that people would not like me if they knew who I really was. *I can't help it that I was raped and abused. My friends would not like me if they knew how I really think.*

I became very sensitive to people not being able to control me. *I will not let Joel control me. I was controlled by Alex growing up. Now that I'm an adult I will not be controlled.*

I realized that I did not know who God was. *Why did God allow Alex to molest me? Why do I have to live with this hell in my life? If God can't keep children safe then what is He doing?*

I believed the counselors and therapists. *My family is very dysfunctional. My Christian "helpers" know what I need. They know how I should deal with my life and my pain.*

Even though I was a minister's wife, my "help" was creating more questions for me than answers. My confusion was increasing. I didn't think it was a problem though because I was doing the culturally accepted thing to deal with problems. I was in Christian counseling and therapy. Was I doing **GOD's *Miracle* Process**?

While I was seeing a therapist I had a strange and unusual experience. The therapy was to help my body relax and make me aware of anything my body "remembered." I began to cry as a variety of thoughts came to my mind.

"No, Daddy, don't do that to me!" Why did Daddy molest me when I was a little girl? He makes me so angry. I hate him too. My life is worse than I thought it was. (Eventually, I learned that Dad never molested me.)

I started telling my family that Dad molested me *until* the day I made a discovery.

You mean it's not true? I only wanted to know the truth about my life. I'll never go to a hypnotist so I'll be safe from Satan's ideas. I don't want him causing any more damage to my life.

I did not know there are other kinds of therapy that can also open my mind for Satan. I learned the hard way. *Any therapy that puts my mind in a state of total openness leaves my mind totally open for Satan.* He put thoughts and pictures in my mind that he wanted me to think.

I knew what my past was and it did not include this story. The devil lied to me about my childhood. He made it much worse than it was.

I believed these thoughts and pictures because I did not know that my new ideas were from Satan. *I thought they were just things I did not remember.*

I did not know Satan worked through these methods of therapy to deceive me. I believed I was safe as long as I got help from Christians and did not go to a hypnotist. Eventually, God showed me how wrong I was.

In reality Dad never touched me or talked to me in any wrong way. Satan wanted to give me another reason to separate myself from Dad.

I didn't know Satan was using "my help" to deceive me and to confuse me more than before I started getting help. I learned and accepted one new concept after another, thinking that this was the process I had to go through for my life to improve. Later I learned this was definitely not **GOD's *Miracle* Process**.

Satan was trying to confuse me through the "Christian" psychology and "Christian" self-help books. Some things I learned were true but most things did not agree with the Bible. I learned that many "Christian" writers and counselors use "New Age" methods and ideas instead of the Bible's methods.

After a few years of therapy, counseling, sharing, and reading, my selfish ideas and fantasies of how people should treat me made me into a very miserable woman. I cut myself off from most of my family and friends. I even divorced Joel and left my church.

I made many decisions and *choices* while I believed New Age ideas. Today, I live with the destructive and permanent consequences of some of those *choices* back then. It's very sad.

My New Age ways of facing my pain, my questions, and my anger brought me to the place that I willingly *chose* to give up almost all the good in my life. The bad parts of my life got much worse than ever before.

Satan was working to isolate me from my God and from people who loved me. He could do more to hurt me as I allowed fewer people to be involved in my life. I had a driving desire to start my life all over again, my way.

The negative and evil experiences and information that were created through my therapy and counseling did not have to happen. It was a rude awakening to realize that Satan had deceived me in all the ways he had. It was hard to accept that Satan can so easily deceive a Christian and a minister's wife.

I learned the hard way that the *Bible gives specific counsel and help for my therapy needs*. The Bible provides answers for every part of my life (II Timothy 3:15-17). This means God will provide the knowledge and comfort for my emotional and psychological needs (Romans 15:4).

The Bible talks about helping me with my pain and confusion after being molested. I never heard anyone tell me that. Of course, these answers are **GOD's** *Miracle* **Process**.

I thank God that I know the Bible is God's most accurate source of healing for my life. Now I can think about my relationships, pain, and anger more the way God thinks. I thank God for His simple answers.

Now I know there are Christian books, therapists, and counselors available that lead people to the *Bible* for God's answers. I could not find this kind of help, so I thought my "help" was better than no help with my life.

"You mean it's not true?" No, I found that most of it is not true if people are not using Bible principles. I continue to thank God that most of the things I learned are not true, especially about my dad. **GOD's** *Miracle* **Process** *replaces Satan's lies* in my mind with Bible truth.

GOD's *Miracle* **Process** has taught me that God's counsel for handling my life does not keep hurting me. God's counsel does not make more problems for me. God's methods of healing have given me understanding I need to function and to be happy.

God's truth brought me back *together* with people that I abandoned. **GOD's** *Miracle* **Process** has produced peace, quietness in my heart, and trust in God (Isaiah 32:17).

It's hard to accept that Satan can so easily deceive a Christian. It's hard to accept that life can be so hard when I didn't know how to follow the Bible's help.

You mean it's not true? How can that be?

I personally discovered that it's easy for things to be untrue. Jesus said that Satan is a deceiver and the father of lies (John 8:44). Jesus said the truth makes me free (John 8:32).

Jesus provides the direction for my life, He always tells me the truth, and gives me reason to live every day (John 14:6). As long as I follow Jesus' counsel I'll know the way to go, I'll know what is true. I won't be deceived, and I'll have quality of life!

God has lots of things He wants me to understand. I really know that God wants me to find relief from my pain and nightmares (Luke 4:18). *How long will it take me to learn what God wants to teach me? Now I see that it totally depends on whether I use God's methods or if I use culturally accepted therapy and counseling.*

I wish I had just asked God to direct me to a safe woman in my church with whom I could have openly shared my pain and my life. If only I had just regularly studied the Bible and prayed with her (Ephesians 6:18). If only I had asked prayer groups to pray for me.

If only I had spent my time doing these things I would have been spared so much agony and my permanent losses. I would not have separated myself from the people that I needed in my life. God would have brought to my mind what I needed to know as I focused on Him (Isaiah 26:3; John 16:13).

Chapter Thirteen

"Mary, your childhood prevented the spiritual part of you from developing normally!"

"Mary, did you hear Me? Did you hear what I told you?"

"Did I hear You? I couldn't miss what You said. I could almost hear Your voice out loud."

"Mary, your childhood prevented the spiritual part of you from developing normally!"

What? Wow! That was God. I've never heard that before. God is going to take me somewhere in my life now with this information.

All three things were true. It was God! It was new information! Now I would be able to continue in **GOD's *Miracle* Process**! I was so excited because now I had help. As fast as it came to my mind I knew I had relief.

I didn't know that the child abuse prevented me from *spiritually* growing up right. I knew that emotionally and sexually I had to re-learn many things. I did not know that I had to re-learn many spiritual things too.

I don't think my therapists and counselors know the answers to my questions about God; what they say makes no sense to me. The rest of my questions, they

71

could make up answers for. This is not working for me anymore. Why don't they know? Not even the pastors I've asked give me answers that help.

Who is God? He let me go through the trauma and tragedy in my life when I was a child. Now that I'm an adult what does God really want to do in my life? Anything? Why did God allow Alex to ruin my life? What is God doing, anyway?

Finally, I admitted to myself that I did not know who God was. I only knew He was not who I'd heard He was all my life. Seriously, why doesn't God stop tragedy and trauma and abuse? Because I could not find the answers I needed about God I finally decided to quit God and church.

If You want me to know who You are God, please tell me. I really do want to know. I still want God's answers. I still believe that God made this world and me, but that's about all I know.

At the same time I decided to quit church and God, I was given inaccurate information about my husband. I decided that Joel was controlling me more than I realized. That would not work for me because my whole childhood was about Alex controlling me. So as a result of this inaccurate information I quit Joel too.

I'll move to where no one knows me. I'll even make up a new last name. I'll just be who I want to be. I won't have to be accountable to anyone. That sounds good for a change. I'll find new friends. I'll find a nice place to live and get another good job. I'll be fine.

I'll have a life that really makes me happy. I won't even have to be a minister's wife anymore. People won't have reasons to expect me to be a certain way. I'll feel I can breathe because Joel, my church, and God will not be controlling me. Oh, yes!

Within five weeks the lawyer had the divorce papers ready. Because my state did not require a separation time before getting divorced, I just signed the papers and it was done for me. After a moving company loaded my belongings, I began my 3,000-mile drive to begin my new life with my new made-up name. I was happy, I thought.

Eight months after I divorced Joel I heard, "Mary, your childhood prevented the *spiritual* part of you from developing normally! Mary, did you hear Me?"

God knew the best time for me to learn. I was now ready for the next steps in **GOD's** *Miracle* **Process**! Hearing from God brought relief to my mind and emotions. I knew God was going to help me even though I was 3,000 miles away from where I belonged.

I got into bed with my Bible, a tablet of paper and pen. I sobbed as I thought about God really helping me. No, I was not as happy with my new life as the enemy wanted me to think that I would be. I was tired of being lonely and living my life on my own. The idea of my new life being fun was only a fantasy put into my mind by Satan.

So, because Alex molested me and raped me, and because adults did not help me deal with my horror when I was a child, I did not grow up spiritually as I should have. Wow! So how in the world does a thirty-eight-year-old woman grow up spiritually now?

"Mary, if you had a little two-year-old daughter and you told her that Jesus loves her, she would believe you

73

just because you told her. She would not ask questions. She would believe you. So that is what you need to do tonight. Believe Me, I love you (Jeremiah 31:3). Hold your questions for Me."

That makes sense. Okay, I'll do that. I'll just believe God loves me because He said He loves me. I'll even hold my questions.

"Good, I'm glad that you accept the fact that I love you. I have given you a gift. The gift is faith. I've given you faith that is at least as big as a mustard seed (Matthew 17:20). This amount of faith makes it possible for you to believe everything I tell you, if you want to have faith in Me. But it's your *choice*. You don't have to believe anything I tell you."

Yes, I do think I have that little bit of faith. I guess that's why I always wanted to know who You are. I'll be the two-year-old growing up now. Thank You, Jesus, for loving me and giving me faith to believe what You tell me. Please take hold of my hand. I'll feel better. You told me to hold my questions, so I will do that. But I'll be glad when I'm old enough to ask.

"Mary, you're old enough now that I can explain some more things to you. You could not understand them very well when you were two, six, or eight years old. You need to understand so pay close attention."

God, I'm listening. Please tell me. I want to know so much. I need to know. I really do not like my life. I feel like I'm hanging on by my fingernails. I've never felt like this before.

"Do you like the fact that I let you *choose* whatever you want? I could have stopped you from *choosing* to divorce Joel, but that was what you wanted to do no matter how devastating it was to him."

I guess that's true. You could have stopped me but I would have been mad at You if You had done that to me. I thought You gave me the right to do whatever I want. I thought I could choose anything I want.

"Mary, you're correct. I did give you that right. You do have that privilege. Guess what? I gave everyone that right, including Alex. I would not stop Alex from making bad *choices* about you anymore than I would stop you from hurting Joel. I know this is new for you to think about."

You got that right. I've never thought about this. No one ever told me this before, but it sure makes sense. Does it say this in the Bible?

"My daughter, being able to *choose* is important. The opposite of *choice* is force and control. You know you don't like force! If I operated the world by force you would be a robot. Robots can not *choose*. I want you to *choose* because then you can *choose* to love Me as I *choose* to love you" (Deuteronomy 30:19, 20; John 15:16).

This is awesome. This is so simple. This is profound to me. God, this really makes me love you. This is good news about my life. I sure do love being able to do what I want!

"So are you glad now that Alex got to make his *choices* about you, even though they were bad *choices?* Remember the terror and trauma?"

Yes, totally. I would rather heal from what Alex did to me than not have the freedom to make my choices. I can get over what Alex did to me. I know You will help me so this abuse will not affect me all my life. The good part is that I will heal and the rest of my life I can make choices! Thank you!

"Mary, you're right. I will help you. Alex's *choices* to molest you and rape you will not affect you badly all your life (Luke 4:18; Matthew 13:15, 16). This is the same thing I have to do for Joel because of the *choices* you made. You know it all but destroyed him. I'll help Joel at his pace.

"I wanted to tell you these things before, but I had to wait until the best time for you (John 16:12). I will never rush you. You can see how I will gently guide you and lead you along" (John 16:13).

God, thank you for being so good at what You do. Spiritually, I feel so close to you because I understand so much more about what You want to do in my life. See, I knew the whole time this is what I needed to know. I just don't know why I had to wait until now for You to tell me. Emotionally I feel so much better. I know that I'm not alone.

"Mary, I will heal you. That is one reason I want to be in your life (Matthew 4:23, 24). Read the Bible. I will help you know how it applies to your needs for healing and recovery. My Word, the Scriptures, are good counsel for every part of your life every day (Romans 15:4; II Timothy 3:16, 17). The Holy Spirit will tell you how to understand the Bible and how to apply the counsel to your life" (I Corinthians 2:13, 14).

God, you are so real to me. This has been so good to hear from You. I wrote it all down so I won't forget. I see that I really do matter to You.

"I'm so glad you mentioned that. Yes, you really do mean a lot to Me, Mary. I made you and I sent Jesus to save you. You are precious to Me" (Isaiah 43:1-5).

I wonder where I will go with You from here. I wonder what You will teach me next. You know I love to learn.

"Mary, don't forget that Satan wants to steal your quality of life. He wants to kill your desire to live and persevere. And he wants to destroy all those good attitudes I put in you (John 10:10). The enemy has been lying to you about so many things" (John 8:44).

I believe that. Now I see how Satan used my counselors, therapists and books to lead me away from my source of true strength and healing. I learned to depend on humans instead of God. I depended so much on myself for solutions. I can see that I was very deceived by the enemy's lies.

I lost so many valuable things in my life because of the lies I believed. It feels so good spiritually, emotionally, and mentally to finally understand these things. I feel relief. I really can see that I must read the Bible and have the Holy Spirit teach me what it means and how it applies to my specific needs.

How long will it take for all this pain to go away and to put my abuse behind me? I know it will depend on how much I depend on God! It will depend on well I follow **GOD's** *Miracle* **Process** instead of the culturally accepted methods of finding "solutions" for my life.

HAVE YOU FORGIVEN HIM?

Chapter Fourteen

"Why are you asking me if I've forgiven him?" I finally had courage to ask my questioner.

I don't like it when people ask me if I've forgiven my brother. He did horrible things to me. Don't they know how traumatic this sexual abuse is for me to deal with?

"Have you forgiven him?"

The nerve of people to ask me if I've forgiven Alex. Do they think it's as easy as brushing my teeth this morning? I guess they don't have a clue what I'm going through now or when I was a little girl.

It really makes me angry when people seem to assume that forgiving Alex ought to be just so easy. Today it feels like I'd have to give up my life if I forgive my terrorizing brother.

"You have to forgive him, you know."

How do people think I could forgive Alex for the atrocities I lived through? Maybe they don't know what it's like to be molested and raped, or to have to show their naked body to whoever may be looking. It's terrifying. What Alex did to me is humiliating.

"Have you forgiven him?"

It makes me angry with people who ask this ridiculous question. It makes me want to shout at them,

78

"Have him do it all to you and see how easy it is for you to forgive him!"

When people talk about forgiving Alex I instantly feel a wall between us. I know they don't understand my pain and trauma because of what they say to me. Don't they know my heart is breaking? Does that matter to them?

I know people love me but why don't they take time to find out what helps me? It seems like they want me to do what makes them comfortable instead of what helps me. They seem to think if I've forgiven Alex then things are better and more comfortable for them. So is this about helping me and my pain, or is this about them and their discomfort?

People probably never meant to be insensitive to how I felt and what I thought. They just truly did not know how to help me. I needed people to feel with me and not judge my feelings. I needed people to think with me and not criticize and censor what I thought.

I needed people to trust God's timing in bringing me to more truth about God's forgiveness. I needed God, not my family and friends, to be my instructor on what to think, how to feel and what I needed to do and when to do it. I needed them just to go with me through **GOD's** *Miracle* **Process** for me.

It was true that in God's time I did need to forgive Alex. God would *guide* me through this forgiveness process. He would not drag me through it. He would not push me (John 16:13).

Learning to forgive was part of **GOD's** *Miracle* **Process** for me. God would have to put it in me to forgive. Every good thing about me is from God

79

(James 1:17). That would include God's gift to me to forgive Alex.

God would also have to give me the gift to *choose* to forgive Alex. Then God gives me another gift and forgives me of all I've done wrong (Ephesians 1:7; Mark 11:26). God taught me that He does not forgive me until I forgive. My willingness to forgive and love as God loves me shows how much I love God (John 13:35).

There was not a chance that I could forgive Alex on my own. Forgiveness for Alex was not in me. I had hate and anger in me. I never wanted to see Alex in my life again.

Why should I forgive my brother for committing such sin and pain against me? What he did to me was very evil. It was very wrong.

In time, God showed me *valuable reasons* to forgive Alex. There would be benefits for me. I just listened to God tell me that I'm a sinner too, and that Alex is not the only one that needs to be forgiven. Most of all, I love my God. I accept His gift of salvation to me and His gift of forgiveness for other people, including Alex.

God helped me understand *my* value to Him (Isaiah 43:1-5). Knowing I am truly valuable to God helped change some things. My anger, hate and resentment because of Alex began to lessen. Understanding my value to God removed some of the fear and pain in my heart.

My warped sense of value from the past was replaced with God's value and love for *me*. Realizing I was so valuable to God actually motivated me to *choose* to forgive Alex. So, one day *I did it*. I took God's gift and *chose* to forgive Alex.

When I *chose* to forgive my brother, he no longer controlled my life. Forgiving Alex helped me by releasing his control from my thoughts and feelings every day.

I don't feel such intense hate for him. I think less about Alex. Now I don't want to talk about my abuse so much. I like thinking more about God now. I have control of my life! It's God's freedom.

When I *chose* to forgive my brother, I allowed Jesus to forgive me for my sins and wrong *choices* (Matthew 6:12). Of course, Jesus had a lot to forgive me for too after living thirty-something years.

If I expect Jesus to choose to forgive me then I had better choose to forgive my brother. Forgiving him does not mean he is right. It just means my conscience is clear from trying to make him responsible to me. He is responsible to God for his choices even though he has traumatized and terrorized my life.

When I *chose* to forgive my brother, I was able to continue with the healing that Jesus wanted to give me. I realized forgiving Alex was all part of **GOD's *Miracle Process*** for me.

I feel like I have more freedom to feel. I can think better. This forgiveness is really liberating! I like this. I am better. The chains of Alex's choices and sin are no longer wrapped around me so tightly. My life does not look so black. Yes, choosing to forgive is choosing freedom.

Choosing to forgive Alex brought more benefits to my life than I could have imagined. I didn't realize that forgiving Alex would change my thinking so much. My *choice* to forgive him and sticking to it everyday, made me a survivor instead of Alex's victim the rest of my life.

Wow. This is amazing. I gain more than Alex when I forgive him. If I tell Alex that I forgive him he will be glad and that's nice. And, if I forgive Alex, I have moved on with my life. Now I'm a survivor not a victim!

If I don't choose to forgive my brother I will be a victim the rest of my life. My childhood abuse will victimize my adult life even without Alex knowing it. That would make me wallowing in my own hurt and pain. No way, I don't want that. Wallowing in the hate makes the pain and disappointment continue. I want to get rid of it forever.

Oh God, thank you for putting it in my heart to choose to forgive my brother. Thank you for releasing him and his sin from my life. Thank you so much because now my abuse and incest are history. Now you and I can work on my present life and not what happened so long ago.

Forgiving Alex did not make all the horror go away at once. God still had thoughts to correct in my mind and He did. There were things that I still misunderstood about myself and my family. There were so many things I misunderstood about relationships in general. In God's time He helped me learn one piece of truth at a time about how life is supposed to function.

I finally learned something I did not expect. God actually helped me genuinely care about this person who all but destroyed my life. I learned that God was making me capable of having compassion for Alex and I began wanting to pray for him and his salvation. I realized that *more* good things happened to me when I prayed for Alex (James 5:16). Wow, God really does know what is good for me.

What happened to Alex that he made such evil choices? Is Alex someone's victim too? I feel bad that my brother has such a messed up life. What? Where did these thoughts come from? His life is much worse than mine. I never even thought of doing such inhumane things to anyone.

I wonder if he'll ever accept Jesus' gift of salvation and be free from the terror that must be in his mind. It would seem pathetic for a person to lose heaven if he wouldn't deal with God and his victim, so he could be in heaven.

I am so thankful that forgiveness is part of **GOD's** *Miracle* **Process** for my life. I have freedom now. *Choosing* to forgive my brother no longer makes me his victim. Forgiving him makes me a *survivor* of sexual abuse and incest.

What Jesus teaches me is the truth. *Choosing* to do what Jesus teaches me to do finally makes me emotionally free and spiritually free to live the way God made to me function (John 8:32). Jesus wants to give me deliverance and healing from the effects of Alex's *choices* (Luke 4:18). Jesus does not want me to live with the damage caused by not forgiving.

The hate and anger were destroying me. My hate and anger were also destroying my husband. It was making our marriage harder. We had many bad memories because of all my challenges.

Jesus prayed for His Father to forgive those who were killing Him because they really didn't understand the results of what they were doing (Luke 23:34). I needed to pray the same prayer.

This prayer does not release people from their own responsibility to God for their *choices*. My brother really did not know what he was doing, either, using the power and control he had. He had his reasons but he did not understand how badly his *choices* would affect my life. God helped me understand so I could sincerely pray this prayer for Alex.

Alex was not the only person I needed to forgive. I needed to forgive *myself*!

My *choices* caused great pain to Joel. Alex was a perpetrator of sexual abuse. I was a perpetrator of abandonment. All abuse is unacceptable and wrong. Trauma has so many similar effects. I hated Alex for what he did to me. Now I saw myself as a perpetrator truly no better than Alex. It's all pain and heartbreak.

How could I do this to Joel? I was so deceived that I did not really understand what I was doing (Luke 23:34). I made terrible, evil *choices* and hurt Joel and so many people.

In order for me to move on with my life I had to allow God to help me *forgive myself* for all the wrong *choices* and pain I caused people (Philippians 3:13, 14). If I don't *choose* to *forgive myself* God does not *choose* to forgive me (Mark 11:26).

Choosing to forgive myself was harder for me than forgiving Alex. I should have had better control of myself and known better. I felt like I was so stupid. I had no responsibility or control over Alex so I did not feel guilty about his *choices*. I just felt guilty about my *choices* and ignorance.

My *choice* to divorce Joel is especially sad because we both loved each other. I didn't know I was deceived about Joel. It has been difficult, but through **GOD's Miracle Process** I have the grace required to *forgive* *myself* and move forward (II Corinthians 12:9)! What a life-changing gift from God (James 1:17).

I am very thankful for the relief and release that *choosing* to forgive has brought to my body, mind and emotions. If I had stubbornly resisted the *choice* to forgive, my life would be so different today. God's ways and methods of dealing with life are always better than my human ways (Isaiah 55:8, 9).

IT'S TIME TO LET IT GO NOW?
Chapter Fifteen

*A*re you sure? It's time to let it go now?
"Mary, you're done. There is nothing left for you to do with the *past*." The thought was so loud in my mind.

What? God, are you sure it's time? You know the kind of person I am. I do not want to prematurely let it go. If it's not time, I'll have to go back and deal with it some more and that would be devastating to me.

"You're done. There is nothing left for you to do with the *past*."

I can hardly believe that it's already time. I knew this time would come but I did not expect it to be this soon.

"You're done. It's over. There's nothing left for you to do that has to do with the *past!*"

It's only been three months since God told me that all the incest, rape, and exhibitionism messed up my spiritual growth. This is fast. I've always believed that someday I would be done working on the past. I never thought I'd always be a "victim." I wanted to be a survivor! Sure enough, God wants me to be a survivor too.

Jesus' truth really does set me free (John 8:32). Thinking and talking about the terror that Alex created in me does not benefit me anymore. I learned what I needed about the *past,* and *now* the time had come to move on. *Now,* bringing up the *past* would be to wallow in Satan's evil for my life. God does not want me to wallow in all that evil (Proverbs 8:13).

Jesus, thank you for helping me understand that You gave Your life for me, Mary. Thank you for telling me how important I am to You, even when emotionally I feel so low (Isaiah 43:1-4).

I've been in an emotional prison for so long. I've been heartbroken all my life. Keeping secrets was so stressful. You've opened my eyes to see that Satan is my real enemy, not Alex (Ephesians 6:12). *He tried to destroy me through Alex's choices.*

There were times I was requested to be where Alex was after God told me I was done working on the *past.* Family reunions were not easy. God had to help me deal with my present life.

I discovered that **GOD's *Miracle* Process** really is a process. It is not an instant zapping. There are so many things I've had to re-learn. So I can move on and not be spiritually and emotionally stuck, God has helped me accept what I cannot change (Philippians 3:13, 14).

Letting the *past* go did many good things for me. It changed my future. Leaving my history behind me meant I would not keep talking about my abuse, unless there was a specific reason.

"Mary, you are cheating your family."

I certainly can't imagine how I am doing that. God, they're not even in my life anymore.

"That's the problem."

During my counseling I removed myself from their lives. That was good because they didn't do what I

87

wanted and they didn't think the way I wanted them to think. I'm better off without them in my life.

"Mary, you're not right. You're treating them worse than you think they're treating you. They did not cut you out of their lives. You think you know how they should be and what they should do. How about treating them the way you want them to treat you (Luke 6:31)?"

My cynicism and criticism of my family is pretty bad. I didn't know that I was cheating them by not letting them love me. God, You really know how to get through to me, don't You? Maybe they don't want me in their lives anymore.

"It's time for you to accept your family for who they are. You need to stop cheating them out of your friendship. I'll help you."

Connecting me with my family was very important to God. He helped make it a smooth transition. I thank each one in my family for their love, help, and encouragement. They have done a lot for me through the years. **GOD's *Miracle* Process** always has helpful surprises!

"Mary, there's something else I have to teach you. People are not accountable to you, they are accountable to Me."

What? God, what did You say?

"Mary, I know people have caused you pain, *but* you have to leave their *choices* with Me. They are accountable to Me, not you."

Wow. I have to make some phone calls.

"Alex, I know we don't understand things the same, but I have to tell you something. There is nothing you've done to me that I will allow to stand in the way of me having a friendship with you that God wants me to have."

That wasn't hard. God gives me strength to follow His counsel (II Corinthians 12:9). *Now I have even more freedom. I'm letting more of the past go! Oh God, you're healing me. Thank you!*

It's true, no matter how much I hurt; people are not accountable to me for what they do to me. They are only accountable to God (Romans 14:12). He's the judge, *not me.*

Letting my past go and releasing Alex to God has given me freedom spiritually and emotionally. Doing what God says helps me to be closer to Him. It has all turned out the way God said it would. His truth about how to deal with my life has set me free in another way (John 8:32).

God has given me the gift of wisdom to be friendly with Alex (James 1:5, 17). God has created the miracle it takes in my heart so I can genuinely care about Alex and the problems he has to deal with (Ezekiel 36:26, 27).

My friendly, forgiving, and positive attitudes toward Alex may encourage him to move forward as God talks to him. Satan is a liar who led Alex to think that what he did to me as a child was good for himself (John 8:44). It has turned out anything but good for Alex.

When God taught me that people are not accountable to me, I also learned I must stop gossiping and talking about people. I needed God to help me with this if I'm serious about going to heaven (Romans 1:29-32). Criticism can be a stumbling block to people and to myself (Romans 14:13).

What? The Doctor says Dad has melanoma cancer and he does not have long to live? No way! I can't imagine. Dad is going to die. I am so thankful that just a few weeks ago I learned that Dad is not accountable to me. God, thank you for helping me release Dad to you. These last few weeks have been special to me because I was not thinking about the past and what I wanted Dad to do and believe. I've had meaningful time with him.

Right after God told me that my parents are accountable to Him, I visited Dad and Mom and celebrated Dad's 81st birthday. Each meal was fun because we had another party. Every time we ate we had more birthday candles and Dad had to open another gift. It lasted all weekend. I did not know that in a couple weeks I would be told that Dad was terminally ill.

God, thank you for telling me about accountability. The enemy could not cheat Dad and me out of my valuable memories. Letting go of the past is what allowed me to have this closeness to Dad, and it means so much to me.

I had made peace in my heart with God and so I could just love Dad as long as I had him. Dad knew I loved him. The enemy had worked hard to turn my heart against Dad but God finally won the battle (Matthew 10:21; Micah 7:6).

I miss Dad. I miss his encouragement. I miss him telling me that he loves me. I have plans to spend eternity with my father. He is resting in the grave waiting for Jesus to call his name. I believe He will stand to his feet and look for his faithful wife and each of his family. He will look for me.

I am so happy that I followed the counsel of my great Counselor (Isaiah 9:6). Because I *chose* to let the *past* go when I first learned about it, I do not have regrets about Dad. If I had waited to be more convinced that

God was right, my experience with my father would have been different.

When I released Dad to God, somehow I no longer felt like I owned Dad. Emotionally, he was not snatched away from me by his death. God prepared me. The last few months I had with Dad were a precious gift from God (James 1:17). Emotionally, God prepared me for my relationship with Dad to end.

All my life Satan was trying to kill, steal, and destroy me, one of Jesus' little lambs (John 10:10). I've been so deceived and made bad *choices*. God understood my motives, my heart.

God knew I was honestly doing the best I could to recover and heal from the abuse. God saw how quick I was to do what I heard Him tell me. He saw I wanted my life to get better.

At age 41, it seemed that God rewarded His little lamb. "Mary, you've worked hard and I want to give you the gift of your dad. I want to give your dad the gift of his daughter."

I remember Dad lying on his bed. His body hurt but he had God's peace in his heart (Isaiah 26:3). Many times while I was holding his hand, I heard Dad say, "Mary, I love you. I love you."

"Thank you, Dad. I love you. You know this is God's miracle! This is what the enemy worked so hard to stop."

"Yes, I know."

God loves re-connecting people. He is so good at it. What a huge gift of God for the heart of a daughter to be re-connected to her father (Malachi 4:6). I praise God for memories I have to think about whenever I want! They are part of **GOD's *Miracle* Process** for me.

Letting the past go has made my life more positive and happy. Emotionally, God brought me out of the black pit that I lived in (Psalm 40:1, 2). *Sexually, I am not a prisoner in my own mind and body* (Luke 4:18). *Letting the past go and not judging people has given me freedom to love people more the way Jesus loves people* (Matthew 5:44, 45; Luke 6:27, 28). *Spiritually, I know God loves me and is working for ME!* (Isaiah 43:1-4).

How could I follow God's counsel? All of God's counsel goes against my character and my nature.

I want people to be accountable to me. I don't want to love people who are not kind to me. I don't even want to be near people who have abused me, lied to me, and harmed me. I certainly don't want to be nice to them. They deserve for me to be nasty to them. I like to gossip. Somehow it makes me feel good.

So how has it been possible for me to change these attitudes? God told me He would give me the gift of a *heart transplant* (Ezekiel 36:26, 27). He would change my attitudes if I would only cooperate with Him and make the *choices* He recommends.

God will give me a new character and make me happy. I am responsible to *choose* His character and give up my hateful and unkind character (Isaiah 61:10; Matthew 5:43, 44).

GOD's *Miracle* Process is about me not wallowing in my abuse, hate, and anger. **GOD's *Miracle* Process** is about me *choosing* to move beyond my *past* and to reach out for the peace and relationships God has for me to experience *now* (Philippians 3:13, 14; Isaiah 32:17).

GOD's *Miracle* Process is about me understanding that Satan is not going to win. Satan is going to be destroyed (Revelation 20:10). I certainly do not want to follow the deceptions, ways, and ideas of the loser!

GOD's *Miracle* **Process** is about me hanging onto God's hand no matter what the enemy brings to my life and then Jesus will save me (Mark 13:13). **GOD's** *Miracle* **Process** is about me believing Him so He can save me (John 3:16).

WHY DO BAD THINGS KEEP HAPPENING TO ME WITH JOEL?

Chapter Sixteen

"Why do bad things keep happening to me? I'm tired of this. What is going on?"

It seems like this is never going to end. It seems like one thing gets better and then another thing gets worse. I do see progress in my life but situations happen that I don't like. I get angry at little things. It's really bad. Does pain ever end?

"Joel, I am so sorry for what I've done to you. I was very wrong to divorce you. God told me some things that I really needed to know, and so I am extremely sorry for all the pain I have caused you. I can't put into words how sorry and remorseful I feel.

"Joel, I do love you. I can't explain just how much I want to be your wife again, but you may not trust me to never leave you again. Joel, knowing about the agony I have caused you causes me more pain than anything Alex ever did to me. Even though it was all logical at the time, I should have known better and not divorced you."

Will Joel ever invite me back home? I know I have to be patient because my choices created this mess. Oh God, please help me to be patient. I just want Joel back. I want "us" back. I never left because I did not love Joel. I did love him and that's why this is so pitiful and pathetic.

After waiting seventeen months for Joel to invite me home, I learned there would be permanent consequences of my *choice* to divorce him. He was going to move on with his life, without me. He was going to be remarried.

No, God, no! I am sorry. Can you make Joel take me back? I just don't want to be without him. This is not fair. I'll do anything it takes.

"Mary, I know you're willing now. But there is a problem. You are willing too late. You have to live with the consequences of your *choices* (Galatians 6:7; II Corinthians 9:6). Joel also gets to *choose*. I know it hurts you. Right or wrong, he's moving on with his life without you.

I don't like this! No wonder Satan wanted to deceive me. God wanted Joel and me together. Joel was part of **GOD's** *Miracle* **Process** *for me. I so willingly gave "us" up. But God's right. Joel gets to choose. I just have to accept Joel's choices. That's the key. I have to accept it. I won't be able to be happy and move on with my life if I keep whining about all of my unnecessary losses (Philippians 3:13, 14). God never wanted me to give up Joel and divorce him.*

"Mary, I'm really sorry. This really is the second time for you to lose Joel. I also feel your pain and disappointment (Isaiah 53:4). You and I will just have to stick together and continue **GOD's** *Miracle* **Process**. I'll do for you what you need" (Matthew 11:28-30).

Alright God, I'll be positive and hold on tight to Your hand. I read in the Bible that You will be my husband

95

(Isaiah 54:5; Jeremiah 3:14). *I feel better knowing that You will help me like I expect from a husband. That is a real gift to me. Thank you so much for telling me how valuable I am to You* (Isaiah 43:1-4).

I really meant it when I told Joel that all the pain I've caused him was hard on me. Honestly, hurting Joel has hurt my heart more than everything Alex did to me. I'm supposed to be in control of myself and not cause such pain. I had to keep *choosing* to forgive myself.

Jesus gave His life to save Joel. Then I made *choices* that created trauma, and tragedy in Joel's life that he never deserved. It is serious for me to hurt people. My abuse does not make it acceptable for me to abuse anyone.

I'm naturally good at hurting people (I Peter 3:8, 9). *I've been hurt so much that I hurt people I don't even need to hurt. I make them feel like me.*

"Mary, you are responsible for your attitudes and your behavior no matter what people do to you (Matthew 7:12). You are to be kind to people and have mercy for them, even when they do what they should not do to you and make wrong *choices* (Luke 6:36, 38). Didn't you want Joel to be kind to you and have mercy for you? If you want to be happy, go do that for Alex, Joel and everyone else!"

Okay, God.

Why do bad things keep happening to me? I sure don't know all the reasons why, but the enemy will steal, kill and destroy me as much as he can (John 10:10).

"Mary, Joel died in his sleep Sabbath morning. The cause of his death is unknown."

I sure didn't expect that phone call.

What? Joel died? Joel is dead? This is the third time to lose him in three years. Jesus, please come soon and take me out of the pain of this evil world. Well, I'm thankful that Joel is not suffering the pain of evil now (Isaiah 57:1). *His battles are over. I do plan to see Joel when I see Dad!*

WHY DO BAD THINGS KEEP HAPPENING TO ME WITH TIM?

Chapter Seventeen

"Why do bad things keep happening to me? I'm so tired of this. What is going on?"

It seems like the pain is never going to end. It seems like one thing gets better and then another thing gets worse. God, thank you for the progress in my life but situations happen that I don't like. I get angry at little things. It's all so bad.

After Joel remarried, I met and married Tim. We met at church. I quickly discovered that my second marriage was harder to adjust to than my first marriage. I took into my second marriage all of my misunderstandings and frustrations about life. I still needed **GOD's *Miracle Process*** to help me.

Tim and I faced many challenges but I really believed God's power could get us through everything (Philippians 4:19). But, it would depend on our *choices* as to how much control we gave God to help us.

Satan was doing all he could to discourage me and make me give up on God. But the more Satan did to me, the more the problems drove me to God this time.

By now I really understand that God is helping me with all my problems. I know that I can stand alone with

98

God on my own two feet. What a big lesson this has been for me. I will not allow my emotions to determine my decisions.

Tim and I went to a minister who did marriage counseling. I was quickly reminded that going to my Counselor in the Bible and listening to the Holy Spirit was safer. The Holy Spirit will not mislead me (John 16:13).

I could see that the counselor's personal issues were greatly influencing his advice. He advised us against doing the work it takes to make a marriage work. He never talked with us about God helping us with our marriage. I had learned too much from God by this time to accept this humanistic approach.

God, this is the second time I've been forced to move out of my home. Our marriage is so off and on. This is not security! I don't know where to go and what to do. I am afraid! Where am I safe? Is there anything I can do to save my marriage? I will not give up on my second marriage like I did my first one.

I called a minister friend and explained the history of our marriage. I asked him if he knew of anything in the Bible that could help me know what *choices* God wanted me to consider regarding my difficult situation with Tim. My friend reminded me of what the Bible says about the freedom to *choose* in I Corinthians 7:15.

Maybe the time has come for me to relate to Tim's choices the way God does. Right or wrong, God respects and accepts his choices. The time may come when it is not respectful to keep trying to make Tim want our marriage.

After talking with God, I knew what I must do. "Tim, I am committed to you. I am still willing to do everything

I can for you and our marriage. But, I must respect your *choices* just as God respects your *choices*."

Two days later I was informed that our marriage was over.

I am such a failure. I feel so embarrassed that my second marriage has failed. People will think I'm a terrible person.

"Mary, some people may think that, but I don't think that way about your marriage. I don't think that way about you. You made your *choices* to make the marriage work. You and I have to accept Tim's *choices* no matter what they are. If he wants to quit he gets to quit."

Really, God? That makes me feel better. Some things Tim says and does make me afraid of him. It has taken courage to tell a few people that I believe my life is in danger. I feel terrible when people don't take Tim's violence seriously. Their disbelief about what he has done to me invalidates my experiences.

What will people say if I don't take Tim serious and I'm found dead? They will say, "Didn't she see it coming? Why didn't she leave?"

Who can I trust? I'm just going to be wise and careful. God, I will listen for Your advice as we go through the divorce!

"Hello, Police Department."

"My name is Mary Taylor. I am so scared. If I am found dead, a divorce is in process."

Joel and I were married almost fifteen years but my marriage with Tim lasted only two and a half years. God, I'm listening for You to tell me what to do now. I'm watching to see how You work out situations for me.

"Mary, learn what you can from these experiences. You know, I'll help you learn more valuable lessons

(Matthew 11:28-30). You know we're in this together. You're not alone" (Matthew 1:23). This is **GOD's** *Miracle* **Process**!

It is so comforting to see how God is helping me move beyond the bad things that happen (Philippians 3:13, 14; John 14:26). *This peace and calm I feel is supernatural.*

WHY DO BAD THINGS KEEP HAPPENING TO ME?

Chapter Eighteen

"Why do bad things keep happening to me? I'm so tired of this. What is going on?"

Some things have gotten better but bad things keep happening. I'm so thankful for the progress God and I are making. I started out learning wrong things about life and relationships because of the abuse. It is good that God is helping me learn the truth about how to relate to people (Isaiah 55:8, 9).

It is very painful to learn what it feels like to be on the other end of *false accusations* and *gossip*. Now I know how people may have felt when they were the subject of my gossip. It is very painful when people do not care enough to personally find out the truth before they gossip.

I should have gone straight to the person I was talking about and learned their facts. But, that might have spoiled part of the satisfaction of gossip.

"Mary, I understand the pain of people telling lies about you and taking sides against you. I certainly know what it's like to have people telling stories about Me that are not even close to the truth (Matthew chapters 26, 27, 28).

Jesus, I know You're right. I guess I've just thought life should be easy and not so painful.

"Sorry, Mary, that is not how life works. As long as you are in this evil world you'll have problems and tribulation (John 16:33). People will treat you however they *choose*. Just stay with Me and I will turn your pain into joy (John 16:20). That's true. I'll do that for you."

God, thank you for patiently helping me understand. Your patience with me feels so good.

"Don't be discouraged about people telling lies about you. Satan tells lies and accuses all of My children about any evil thing (Revelation 12:10). The devil is angry with all my children" (Revelation 12:12).

Okay, God, I get it, these accusations about me are really caused by Satan. The devil is such a devil. He puts all kinds of hateful things into our heads. So it's Satan that I really need to be mad at for all these problems I have to deal with! When I think about my pain this way, it doesn't hurt quite so bad (Ephesians 6:12).

"You're learning. You're doing well. Just expect to be persecuted because you are doing what I counsel you to do. Remember, you have a big reward waiting for you in heaven when Jesus comes" (Matthew 5:10-12).

GOD's *Miracle* Process is never ending. He just keeps doing what He is so good at (John 14:26)! God wants me to accomplish good things in my life even though I was abused (John 15:16). This is what **GOD's *Miracle* Process** is about.

Why do bad things keep happening to me? Maybe my own choices have created part of my own problems. Maybe not all of my problems are caused by other people.

My brain was set up for *failure* and *loss* as a result of the abuse. My body, brain, and emotions were molested and raped.

I kept trying to save myself but I was not successful. I could not make Alex stop. I was always losing my battles.

"Mary, I will help you think about success instead of failure and defeat. You can do anything because I'm helping you (Mark 10:27; Philippians 4:13). I will help you think about your life as productive and positive."

Okay, God. I want to think positive about what You want me to do. It's exciting to think I can do anything, anything You want me do! No, You have not abandoned me.

My brain was set up for *abandonment.* I was molested without Dad and Mom to help save me. I always knew the abuse was wrong and because people did not help me I felt physically and emotionally abandoned.

Why don't people help me? They act like they like me, so why don't they help me? I hate what Alex did to me. My secrets make me feel alone even though my family is with me.

God is not abandoning me; instead He is leading me through **GOD's *Miracle* Process** (Psalm 23:2, 3).

My brain was set up to *escape* people and situations that would hurt me. My brain knew I needed to escape the abuse, but I couldn't. My brain quickly analyzed every situation. Every abusive experience required a huge amount of energy. At a young age, my mind was put in "escape" mode.

As an adult, I've needed to escape some situations I've been in. But I was confused thinking I just wanted to run and cop out.

It's been important for God to help me with my "escape" mode. As an adult, there was a time God was providing a way for me to escape from a bad situation, but I could not hear Him. My old way of thinking told me, "Again, you just want to run away from it."

God had to use someone else to help me see what He wanted me to do. I prayed about my advice, and sure enough, my "escape" issue kept me from being able to hear God telling me, "Go, I don't want my daughter living like this."

How can I keep bad situations from happening? How can I make each situation end sooner? Thinking like this all the time is exhausting! So often my life feels like my hand is on a hot burner.

God is helping me learn that there is a difference between the sanity of taking my hand off a hot burner and escaping or running away from situations I don't like. It's true that God creates ways to remove me from situations He does not want me in (I Corinthians 10:13).

So, as I listen to Him talk to me and I leave my life in God's hands, He will arrange for me what He wants me to do. **GOD's *Miracle* Process** is teaching me the big difference between me *escaping,* and *listening* to God tell me He has an escape for me.

My brain was also taught to *not trust*. My brain was taught to do what I could to *protect myself* from more pain and damage from people.

No one is saving me from my problems, so I will have to be tough. I will have to figure out on my own how to survive.

God taught me that when I was a child, I needed adults to help me. Now, as an adult, if people make bad *choices,* God will be the one to help me. God and I together will do what needs to be done to take care of me. I need to trust God, and people who are trustworthy.

As I listen to God's advice, He will help me and sustain me (Psalm 55:22). As I let God lead me, He will shelter me and keep me safe from the enemy (Psalm 61:3).

I discovered that methods I used as a child to help me cope usually did not work as well for me as an adult.

As I understand what my brain has been taught, I can see if I fall into these patterns in my every day situations as an adult. I must determine why I react to things like I do.

"Mary, if you want less pain, you must understand what I'm telling you about how your brain was trained. You really do create a lot of your pain because of the way you relate to things. The ways you thought as a child are not the best ways to deal with life" (Isaiah 55:7-9).

Okay, God, I'm listening.

This is a big key in **GOD's *Miracle* Process** with me. God and I have to re-train my brain. I have to make *choices* about how I will react and respond to things I like or don't like.

What mode am I operating from? Am I protecting myself from physical and emotional danger? Am I trying to escape a painful situation? Am I afraid of losing so I give it up before it's taken from me? Do I want to walk out of a bad situation before I am abandoned?

These attitudes and actions sabotaged many friendships and relationships. My attitudes and actions kept people at a comfortable distance for me. I allowed people to love me only as much as I wanted. If I saw problems in a relationship I would end it before someone else *chose* to end it. That way I had a sense of control and hoped I would be hurt less.

A protective attitude keeps people at a distance, so that I feel safe. People can only get as close as I allow. But, keeping my spouse at a "safe" distance does not allow us to be as intimate as we need to be.

I can't have friendships with people the way God wants when I keep people at my comfortable distance. God, I see this can be very harmful to me in being able to create long-term relationships. Thank you for this lesson.

Learning why I react the ways I do is necessary to changing my behavior. I make better *choices* when I understand the reasons why I'm quick to react. **GOD's** *Miracle* **Process** fits in right here.

It seems like I usually don't react the way I want to, or the way I should. Each time I make a mess and get all stressed out I have to review my wrong choices and see where I began to go wrong.

The Holy Spirit patiently guides me into showing me how I would have been wise to respond and *choose* differently (John 16:13). The outcome of the situation would have been better and more the way I wanted. So next time I can practice what the Holy Spirit taught me.

I have to be patient with myself because it takes time to make new habits. I have to slow down and think when situations happen. I have to choose what my response will be instead of reacting like I usually do. Slow down! Pray! Think! Choose!

I am so thankful for **GOD's** *Miracle* **Process**. God is patient with me as I'm trying to put into practice what He teaches me. I have to be patient with myself.

I cannot change my brain immediately. It was years of practice that created the bad reactions and it is practice and the power of God that creates good and positive responses (Acts 1:8; John 1:12).

As a child, I was forced to take on unfair responsibilities. But now, as an adult, I am *responsible* to *choose* to work with the Holy Spirit and re-learn what I need to learn. God does not allow me to cop out with, "I was treated badly so it does not matter how I destroy myself or people around me" (Romans 12:21; I Peter 3:8, 9).

GOD's *Miracle* Process *really makes a difference. The longer I listen to the Holy Spirit and do what He guides me to do, I see that I'm creating fewer stressful and bad situations. If I don't continually listen to God, I will be my own enemy as I sabotage and destroy the good in my life. As I listen to the Holy Spirit I can control how much bad I create (John 14:6)!*

A teachable and humble attitude makes me more peaceful and happy (Matthew 5:5; Proverbs 1:33). As I submit myself to God and do what He asks, I have a quietness and peace in my heart. God gives me total assurance that everything is going to be alright as I follow His counsel (Isaiah 32:17).

God is not done with me. I do not have His permission to make up my own solutions, like I used to do. He is going to keep working with me on **GOD's *Miracle* Process** until Jesus comes to take me home (Philippians 1:6). God is teaching me to tightly hold His hand and He will provide solutions for *me*.

MY CHILD, YOU ARE A SURVIVOR!

Chapter Nineteen

"**M**y child, you are a survivor! You are not a victim of the enemy. You are a survivor because you are holding on to Me. I am so proud of you."

Wow! That is special. God is proud of me!

"Mary, Satan is My enemy. A battle has been going on between him and Me. I want to explain some of the story to you.

"I created angels in heaven. The highest executive angel was Lucifer (Isaiah 14:12). He was not happy with His job description. He became jealous that he did not have the same authority as Me, his Creator.

"Lucifer decided the best way to get more power was to do character assassination on Me. He told the angels all kinds of things about Me that were not true. This was so they would think and do what he wanted. Lucifer actually convinced one third of the angels that his stories about Me were true (Revelation 12:4).

"Can you believe it, Mary? There really was war in heaven (Revelation 12:7). But you can see Who won! I am still in heaven! Lucifer and the rebellious angels could not stay in heaven. They were sent to earth to live (Revelation 12:7-9). Their attitudes of independence, jealousy, and criticism made heaven anything but peaceful.

"Lucifer, the executive angel, had a big character change. He became the devil, Satan, a deceiver, and your accuser (Revelation 12:9, 10). His character changed because of his attitudes. Lucifer thought He was going to be better and more powerful than Me (Isaiah 14:12-14).

"Adam and Eve were the first two people I made on this earth, to enjoy more pleasure than you can imagine. Every day I used to take time to walk side by side with Adam and Eve. All three of us looked forward to our time together because it meant so much to us" (Genesis 3:8, 9).

God, they were so fortunate to be with You like that. Why can't I do that?

"I'll get to the answer of your question in a minute. As a result of the war in heaven, Satan and all the rebellious angels were here on earth with Adam and Eve. As soon as he could, Satan tempted Adam and Eve and each of My children to follow his ideas.

"I must know if each person is safe for Me to take to heaven when Jesus returns. Will My children *choose* to have a *loyal attitude* toward Me because I love them and created them or will they *choose* to have an *independent and rebellious attitude* toward Me? Rebellion is not an acceptable attitude for peace in heaven.

"I set up a test for Adam and Eve. They could eat from all the trees where they lived except one. I had to test them to see if they would be loyal to Me or to My enemy, Satan (Genesis 2:15-17).

"First, Eve did not pass her test, and then Adam did not pass his test (Genesis 3:1-7). Mary, I cannot begin to explain how badly I felt. I came looking for My children. They felt so guilty and so much shame for what they had done that they were actually hiding from Me when I found them" (Genesis 3:8).

I know what that's like. I've done that many times. I don't like feeling guilt and shame.

"Well, we had a long chat (Genesis 3:9-19). I shared My heart with them. I told them they would experience consequences for their *choices*. One consequence would be that they would die (Genesis 3:19).

"I also made a promise to Adam and Eve. I told them that I loved them so much that I already had a plan for them to be saved with Me in heaven (Genesis 3:15). Jesus would *choose* to *give* His life to save all of My children (John 3:16).

"One reason I was so sad about the consequences of their *choices* was the fact I did not walk with them every day. Sin separates.

"Sin separates Me from My children (Isaiah 59:2). I don't like that. Instead of us talking face to face, Adam and Eve learned to pray. Each time Adam and Eve turned away from their rebellious *choices* and wanted to talk with Me, I always listened (II Chronicles 7:14). Mary, this is the kind of relationship I want with you, every day!"

God, I can't imagine how bad you really felt not being able to go for walks with Adam and Eve.

"Satan was so happy that he got Eve and Adam to *choose* what he offered them. Now he was able to keep tempting them.

"It is the result of this story that you have been dealing with in your life. Mary, because I want you to be with Me in heaven, I also have to test you to see to whom you will be loyal. Don't forget this."

Serious? You really make up tests for me?

"Satan has so much anger for Me that he also hates My children. Who I love, he hates. Because I love you, Satan hates you (Revelation 12:12). Satan knows that when you hurt, I hurt! He loves hurting Me. This is one reason why he tempts you and hurts you.

"The devil wants you to *choose* bad things so you will be hurt and so you will hurt others. The devil wanted Alex to *choose* bad things to destroy himself and you (John 10:10).

"When you suffer, Satan wants you think that I should have stopped your pain that he causes. My job is to be with You (Matthew 1:23). My job is to help you deal with the pain and its effects (Luke 4:18).

"Satan made it his job to deceive you and to make you think he's not the one causing the evil, trauma, and tragedy in your life (Revelation 12:9). Remember, Satan lies to you like he did to Eve (John 8:44). He does this to all My children."

I've heard a lot of Satan's lies. I've been so deceived and influenced by him.

"Mary, Jesus died for you so you and I can have the gift of being face to face in heaven (I Thessalonians 5:9, 10). The blood of Jesus makes you clean from all your rebellious attitudes and sin (I John 1:7). If you confess your independent attitudes and sin to Me I will forgive you" (I John 1:9).

*God, You and I will be together face to face! Then, **our miracle process** will be done!*

"Each human being is My child. Mary, stay close to Me. You're a survivor. When Jesus comes back you will be confident where you have placed your loyalty and you will not be ashamed of your *choices* (I John 2:28). I can hardly wait to be face to face with all My children. Do you see the value I place on you?"

This story is so encouraging. I can see that You've been through a lot, not just me.

"I told you the beginning of the story but now I have to finish My story for you. The ending is great! Jesus came to earth once, but He's going to come back again and take you home with Him (John 14:1-3). The important thing is that Jesus can only take home those who do what I ask them to do (Matthew 7:21-23). This is the only way it works.

"Like I already mentioned, My children must be loyal to Me. They cannot live with Me and have an independent and rebellious attitude toward Me.

"After you are home with Jesus and Me, Satan will be destroyed (Revelation 21:10). Yes, forever destroyed! Satan will never be able to tempt you again. Sin will be destroyed. Trauma, tragedy, torture, pain, anger, and sin will never exist again" (Nahum 1:9).

This is certainly good news! I definitely like this part of the story. Satan will be destroyed! YES!

"Mary, see why you must pass your tests? See how important the consequences of your *choices* are to Me? The separation of sin is so painful to Me. I will never be separated again from you and all My children who love Me, and who are loyal to Me. You will never be tested again. You will have made your final decision to be loyal to Me!"

God, I am looking forward to my last test!

"Mary, Jesus is going to wipe away your last tears (Revelation 21:4). That is true. The *choices* that have brought tragedy and pain into your life will all be gone, forever. Your *choices*, Alex' *choices*, and everyone's *choices* will no longer badly affect your life. The sad and painful parts of your life will be totally gone."

Jesus is going to wipe my tears from my face? Both of You are so compassionate and loving to me. You've done so much to help me through all the tragedies in my life.

"I am so happy to tell you that all the effects of the abuse you've suffered will no longer affect you. Have courage now because you will have complete freedom from the abuse. You will never think about it again. All your bad memories will be gone from your mind (Revelation 20:4). I'm going to make everything brand new for you (Revelation 20:5).

"Mary, My dear child, you are a *survivor.* I am so proud of you. You are listening to Me and you're *choosing* to allow Me to help you with your life. This is what makes you a survivor and not a victim of the enemy.

"Keep talking with me (II Chronicles 7:14). One day you and I will be together face to face enjoying the pleasures I have waiting for you" (Revelation 21:3).

Thank you, God, for telling me this story. Thank you for **OUR** *Miracle* **Process** *together. Thank you for all Your counsel, it makes such a difference in my happiness every day. My life has improved so much since I've been listening to Your counsel for me.*

The last five years I've been working to help people choose *to live forever with You. I love doing that for You! And God, with Your direction I've started* **Choices International***. You want me help people know they have more* choices *than they may realize so that You* *can improve the quality, value, and purpose of their lives too.*

Thank you for telling me that I am Your daughter, and Your survivor of the enemy. Thank you for loving me. I give You my loyalty! I am waiting for Jesus to come and take me home to be with You, forever! Thank you, with all my heart!

Chapter Twenty

My appreciation for You will always be what I talk about (Psalm 34:1).

You have delivered me from fear that the enemy tries to put in me to keep me from being happy and *choosing* to do things that are good for me to do (Psalm 34:4).

I *choose* to not be ashamed about my childhood and my history (Psalm 34:5).

Thank you for assigning an angel to stay with me every day to help me (Psalm 34:7).

I know from experience that my life is better when I *choose* to do what you counsel me to do and when I *choose* to believe You (Psalm 34:8).

I've learned that when I listen to You and do what You tell me to do, I will not lack anything in my life that is good for me (Psalm 34:9; Psalm 84:11).

Thank you for inviting me to come to You and for offering to be my teacher (Psalm 34:11).

I *choose* to speak good about people instead of what I don't like about them (Psalm 34:13).

I *choose* to follow Your advice and be at peace, and stay away from the evil that is around me (Psalm 34:14).

Thank you for watching what is happening to me and for listening to me because You care about *my* life (Psalm 34:15).

Thank you so much for hearing my cries for help and for protecting me (Psalm 34:17).

Thank you for *choosing* to be close to me and saving me with you, forever (Psalm 34:18).

Thank you for telling me that life will not be easy but that You will keep helping me, no matter what the enemy tries to do to me (Psalm 34:19).

Thank you for telling me up front what will happen to my life if I continually *choose* the ways of the enemy (Psalm 34:16, 21).

Thank you for *choosing* to save me from the hell Satan would like to create in my life today, and for providing all my needs today and forever (Psalm 34:22).

God, You have been an excellent teacher. Thank you for your patience, and going over the same lessons as often as I need it. I'm so happy that I can see progress in **my *Miracle* Process with YOU!**

GOD's *MIRACLE* PROCESS *BENEFITS*
Chapter Twenty-One

The benefits of **GOD's** *Miracle* **Process** are not available anywhere else, except from God (John 3:27). I have discovered that it is wise to remember often that listening to God offers us many benefits.

God offers us forgiveness for our wrong *choices* (Psalm 103:3). But, in order for God to forgive us we have to accept His gift of forgiveness, and *choose* to forgive people who have made wrong *choices* against us (Mark 11:26). Then God can offer us the benefit of those people being released from our lives.

God offers us healing for our wounded and broken hearts (Psalm 103:3). God offers us healing for our minds by *choosing* to believe and do what Jesus taught (Luke 5:17).

God offers us safety for our lives now and forever (Psalm 103:4). *Choosing* to respect God's counsel offers us safety and confidence, and keeps us from the traps of Satan (Proverbs 14:26, 27). God offers us life face to face with Him forever when we *choose* to believe what He tells us, and when we *choose* to follow His counsel (John 3:36).

God offers us love and kindness for people, especially for those who seem to not deserve it (Psalm 103:4).

God offers us the opportunity to *choose* to care about people the way we'd like them to care about us (Romans 12:10).

God offers us mercy and compassion for people who have made wrong *choices* that have hurt our hearts (Psalm 103:4). God offers us the *choice* to have mercy and compassion for people, which makes a big difference in our lives and theirs (Jude 21, 22).

God offers us satisfaction and fulfillment with good things (Psalm 103:5; Joel 2:26). God offers us the gift to restore to us, later in our lives, what we should have had when we were children and young adults (Psalm 103:5; John 2:25). Full restoration will come when we are with Him face to face in heaven.

Jesus came to provide many benefits that are part of **GOD's *Miracle* Process** for His children.

Jesus said, "The Holy Spirit of My Father is upon Me, because He has important and valuable things for Me to do for you, My child.

"The Holy Spirit anointed Me to preach the gift of salvation and His genuine love to people who are emotionally and spiritually drained, poor, and bankrupt.

"I was sent to heal your pain, anger, and broken heart.

"I came to teach you how to have relief and to rescue you from what holds you captive, emotionally and spiritually.

"I came to be your Counselor, so we can discuss the things in your life you don't understand, and what to do about them.

"I came to heal your heart, which has been emotionally, mentally, and spiritually bruised, battered, and traumatized.

"I also came to heal your body, which has been sexually and physically abused and beaten. This is **GOD's *Miracle* Process** that I was sent to do with you" (Luke 4:18 paraphrased by Mary J. Taylor, pseudonym).

GOD's *Miracle* Process provides other benefits that we need to not take for granted.

"God does not give you the attitude of fear; fear comes from the enemy. God gives you His power and teaches you what true love is. **GOD's *Miracle* Process** in your life is to keep your mind stable from the brainwashing and trauma of the enemy" (II Timothy 1:7 paraphrased by Mary J. Taylor, pseudonym).

GOD's *MIRACLE* PROCESS *SUMMARY*
Chapter Twenty-Two

T hroughout my childhood, God was busy helping His little girl survive her trauma and tragedies even though I did not know about **GOD's** *Miracle* **Process**. I lived through many years of being a confused and angry adult, yet God lived with me and was busy helping me with **GOD's** *Miracle* **Process**.

Satan has provided lots of opportunities for me to see if I would *choose* to listen to him, or if I would *choose* to trust God since I've learned that God has a *Miracle* **Process** for me. Sometimes I have made *choices* according to God's counsel, and sometimes I have made *choices* that were traps of the enemy. I will mess up if I don't continually *choose* to listen to God's counsel, and follow it.

"God, I've tried to patiently wait for **YOUR** *Miracle* **Process** in my life. You've seen my tear stained face, my heart wrenching trauma and pain, abuse and fear. You carefully heard all my confusion and questions, and listened every time I cried" (Psalm 40:1 paraphrased by Mary J. Taylor, pseudonym). I'm sure God's face was tear stained too by all He saw happen to me!

"**YOUR Miracle Process** brought me up and out of a hole that felt black, horrifying, and terrorizing. **YOUR Miracle Process** has placed my mind and emotions on You, my Rock, so now I have a firm foundation. My *choice* to trust and believe in You really makes me feel grounded. I *choose* to follow Your counsel for my life each day" (Psalm 40:2 paraphrased by Mary J. Taylor, pseudonym).

"**YOUR Miracle Process** of love and healing has put a new and different song in my heart, including praise to You for Your power to change my life. God, it's just so personal to me. People see I'm a survivor (not a victim), and how You've helped me. They're amazed and respect You for it. As people witness Your life-changing power in my life, many are *choosing* to trust You to change their lives too" (Psalm 40:3 paraphrased by Mary J. Taylor, pseudonym).

Someday, **GOD's *Miracle* Process** with me, and **GOD's *Miracle* Process** with you will be *finished!* Jesus will come back from heaven and it's our *choice* and privilege to live with Him face to face forever (John 14:1-3). Life with its pain, abuse, trauma, and tragedy will never happen again (Nahum 1:9). Just imagine, living in the same town with God. You can; YOU are His *transformed* and *treasured* child!

GOD's *MIRACLE* PROCESS *PROMISES*
Chapter Twenty-Three

*G*od has made many promises to His children and that includes you. **GOD's *Miracle* Process** helps you choose to do your part, and then God is able to do His part with YOU!

- God gave His only Son to give you the *gift of living with Him* forever (John 3:16).

- God invites you to come to Him. He *accepts you* and will not reject you (Matthew 11:28).

- God *created* you, God *redeemed* you, and you *belong to GOD* (Isaiah 43:1).

- God will give you a new, *healthy attitude* about what you've been through (Ezekiel 36:26, 27).

- God will *guide* you into only things that are *true* and give you *answers* and *counsel* for what you're dealing with (John 16:13).

- God will give you *peace, quietness* and *assurance* in your mind if you do what He asks and follow His counsel (Isaiah 32:17).

- God will give you *strength, sustain* you, and *help* you (Isaiah 41:10).

- The Bible is to give you *comfort* and *hope* (Romans 15:4).

- God will give you *peace* if you keep your mind thinking about Him (Isaiah 26:3).

- God will give you *rest* if you take your questions, issues, situations, and each of your problems to Him (Matthew 11:28-30).

- God will *provide* for your material needs (Matthew 6:31-33). Ask God (John 14:13).

- God loves you and God will *provide people* to help you (Isaiah 43:4).

- God will help you live *safely* and quiet your mind from your fears (Proverbs 1:33).

- God will *destroy your sorrow and pain*. God Himself will wipe away your last *tears* (Revelation 21:4).

- God *forgives* you as you are willing to *forgive* those who wrong you (Luke 6:37).

- God *forgives* you of *all* your sin (I John 1:9).

- God will give you *healing* and *recovery* if you follow His *counsel* (Luke 4:18).

- *God will rebuke Satan for you* so Satan will not be able to destroy you (Malachi 3:10, 11).

- God does *not change* on you (Malachi 3:6).

- *God is always with you* (Matthew 28:20).

- Jesus is coming soon with His reward for you because you did not quit. You will not be here forever (John 14:2, 3; Revelation 22:12).

ADDITIONAL READING

New Testament of the Bible: Matthew, Mark, Luke, John

Old Testament of the Bible: Psalms, Proverbs

A Trip Into the Supernatural, by Roger Morneau [Hagerstown, MD, Review & Herald Publishing, 1982, 1993]

Before You Say "I Do," by H. Norman Wright and Wes Roberts [Eugene, OR, Harvest House Publishers, 1977, 1997]

Child Sexual Abuse, by Maxine Handcock and Karen Maines [Wheaton, IL, Harold Shaw Publishing, 1987]

Communication, Key to Your Marriage, by Norm Wright [Ventura, CA, Regal Books, 1979]

Dear Nancy: a trusted advisor gives straight answers to questions about marriage, sex, and parenting, by Nancy L. Van Pelt with Madlyn Lewis Hamblin [Nampa, ID, Pacific Press Publishing, 2005]

Desire of Ages, by Ellen G. White [Nampa, ID, Pacific Press Publishing, 1898, 1940]

Epidemic: how teen sex is killing our kids by Meg Meeker [Washington D.C., Life Line Press, 2002]

Every Man's Battle, by Stephen Arterburn, Fred Stoeker, Mike Yorkey [Colorado Springs, CO, WaterBrook Press, 2000]

Healing of Memories, by David Seamands [Wheaton, IL, Victor Boos, 1985]

How to Get Your Teen to Talk to You, by Connie Grigsby and Kent Julian [Sisters, OR, Multnomah Publishing, 2002]

In Search of Pearls: Restoration After Child Abuse, A Thing of Beauty, by Sharon Estrada [Columbus, GA, Brentwood Christian Press, 1997]

Messages to Young People, by Ellen G. White [Hagerstown, MD, Review & Herald Publishing, 1930, renewed 1958]

Mind, Character and Personality, Volumes 1 and 2, by Ellen G. White [Hagerstown, MD, Review and Herald Publishing, 1977, 2000]

Ministry of Healing, by Ellen G. White [Nampa, ID, Pacific Press Publishing, 1903]

Never Good Enough, by Carol Cannon [Nampa, ID, Pacific Press Publishing, 1993]

Sins of the Father, by Marianne Morris [Nampa, ID, Pacific Press Publishing, 1993]

Smart Love, by Nancy L. Van Pelt [Grand Rapids, MI, Fleming H. Revell, 1997, 2001]

Steps to Christ, by Ellen G. White [Nampa, ID, Pacific Press Publishing, 1892, 1908]

Straight Talk: How Teens Can Make Wise Choices About Love & Sex, by Loretta Parker Spivey [Hagerstown, MD, Review & Herald Publishing, 2000]

The Adventist Home, by Ellen G. White [Nampa, ID, Pacific Press Publishing, 1952]

The Great Controversy, by Ellen G. White [Nampa, ID, Pacific Press Publishing, 1888, 1907]

The Five Love Languages, by Gary Chapman [Chicago, IL, Northfield Publishing, 1992, 1995, 2004]

The Language of Love, by Gary Smalley and John Trent, Ph.D. [Denver, CO, Focus on the Family Publishers, 1988]

Where Is God When Bad Things Happen?, by Horace O. Duke [St. Meinrad, IN, Abbey Press, 1991]

SCRIPTURE REFERENCES

All Scripture quotations are taken from the New King James Version of The Holy Bible [Nashville, Camden, New York, Thomas Nelson Publishers].

II Chronicles 7:14 God said, "If My people who are called by My name will humble themselves, and pray and seek My face, and turn from their wicked ways, then will I hear from heaven, and will forgive their sin and heal their land." Chapter Nineteen

I Corinthians 2:13, 14 These things we also speak, not in the words which man's wisdom teaches but which the Holy Spirit teaches, comparing spiritual things with spiritual. But the natural man does not receive the things of the Spirit of God, for they are foolishness to him; nor can he know them, because they are spiritually discerned. Chapter Thirteen

I Corinthians 7:15 But if the unbeliever departs, let him depart; a brother or a sister is not under bondage in such cases. But God has called us to peace. Chapter Seventeen

I Corinthians 10:13 No temptation has overtaken you except such as is common to man; but God is faithful, who will not allow you to be tempted beyond what you are able, but with the temptation will also make the way of escape, that you may be able to bear it. Chapter Eighteen

II Corinthians 9:6 …He who sows sparingly will also reap sparingly, and he who sows bountifully will also reap bountifully. Chapter Sixteen

II Corinthians 12:9 Jesus said, "… My grace is sufficient for you, for My strength is made perfect in weakness…" Chapter Eight, Fourteen, Fifteen

Deuteronomy 30:19, 20 God said, "… Choose life, that both you and your descendants may live, that you may love the Lord your God, and that you may obey His voice, and that you may cling to Him, for He is your life and the length of your days…" Chapter Thirteen

Ephesians 1:7 In Him we have redemption through His blood, the forgiveness of sins, according to the riches of His grace. Chapter Fourteen

Ephesians 6:12 For we do not wrestle against flesh and blood, but against principalities, against powers, against the rulers of the darkness of this age, against spiritual hosts of wickedness in the heavenly places. Chapter Fifteen, Eighteen

Ephesians 6:18 Praying always with all prayer and supplication in the Spirit. Chapter Twelve

Ezekiel 36:26, 27 God said, "I will give you a new heart and put a new spirit within you; I will take the heart of stone out of your flesh and give you a heart of flesh. I will put My Spirit within you and cause you to walk in My statutes, and you will keep My judgments, and do them." Chapter Fifteen

Galatians 6:7 Do not be deceived, God is not mocked; for whatsoever a man sows, that he will also reap. Chapter Sixteen

Genesis 2:15-17 Then the Lord God took the man and put him in the garden of Eden to tend and keep it. And the Lord God commanded the man, saying, "Of every tree of the garden you may freely eat, but of the tree of the knowledge of good and evil you shall not eat,

for in the day that you eat of it you shall surely die."
Chapter Nineteen

Genesis 3:1-3 Now the serpent was more cunning than any beast of the field which the Lord God had made. And he said to the woman, *"Has* God indeed said, 'Ye shall not eat of every tree of the garden'?" And the woman said unto the serpent, "We may eat of the fruit of the trees of the garden; but of the fruit of the tree which is in the midst of the garden, God hath said, 'You shall not eat it, nor shall you touch it, lest you die.'" Chapter Nineteen

Genesis 3:4, 5 And the serpent said to the woman, "You will not surely die. For God knows that in the day you eat of it your eyes will be opened, and you will be like God, knowing good and evil." Chapter Nineteen

Genesis 3:6, 7 And when the woman saw that the tree was good for food, and that it was pleasant to the eyes, and a tree desirable to make one wise, she took of its fruit and ate. She also gave to her husband with her, and he ate. Then the eyes of both of them were opened, and they knew that they were naked; and they sewed fig leaves together and made themselves coverings. Chapter Nineteen

Genesis 3:8, 9 And they heard the sound of the Lord God walking in the garden in the cool of the day, and Adam and his wife hid themselves from the presence of the Lord God among the trees of the garden. Then the Lord God called to Adam and said to him, "Where are you?" Chapter Nineteen

Genesis 3:10-12 So he said, "I heard Your voice in the garden, and I was afraid because I was naked; and I hid myself." And he said, "Who told you that you were naked? Have you eaten from the tree of which I commanded you that you should not eat?" And the man said, "The woman whom You gave to be with me, she gave me of the tree, and I ate." Chapter Nineteen

Genesis 3:13 And the Lord God said to the woman, "What is this you have done?" And the woman said, "The serpent deceived me, and I ate." Chapter Nineteen

Genesis 3:14, 15 So the Lord God said to the serpent, "Because you have done this, you are cursed more than all cattle, and more than every beast of the field; on your belly you shall go, and you shall eat dust all the days of your life. And I will put enmity between you and the woman, and between your seed and her Seed; He shall bruise your head, and you shall bruise His heel." Chapter Nineteen

Genesis 3:16, 17 To the woman He said, "I will greatly multiply your sorrow and your conception; in pain you shall bring forth children; your desire shall be for your husband, and he shall rule over you." Then to Adam He said, "Because you have heeded the voice of your wife, and have eaten from the tree of which I commanded you, saying, 'You shall not eat of it: cursed is the ground for your sake; in toil you shall eat of it all the days of your life.'" Chapter Nineteen

Genesis 3:19 God said, "In the sweat of your face you shall eat bread till you return to the ground, for out of it you were taken; for dust thou are, and to dust you shall return." Chapter Nineteen

Hebrews 4:15 Speaking of Jesus, "For we do not have a High Priest who cannot sympathize with our weaknesses, but was in all points tempted as we are, yet without sin." Chapter Two

Isaiah 9:6 For unto us a Child is born, unto us a Son is given; and the government will be upon His shoulder. And His name will be called Wonderful, Counselor, Mighty God, Everlasting Father, Prince of Peace. Chapter Fifteen

Isaiah 14:12-14 How you are fallen from heaven, O Lucifer, son of the morning! How you are cut down to the ground, you who weakened the nations! For you have said in your heart, "I will ascend into heaven, I will exalt my throne above the stars of God; I will sit also on the mount of the congregation on the farthest sides of the north. I will ascend above the heights of the clouds, I will be like the Most High." Chapter Nineteen

Isaiah 26:3 You will keep him in perfect peace, whose mind is stayed on You, because he trusts in You. Chapter Seven, Twelve, Fifteen

Isaiah 32:17 God said, "The work of righteousness will be peace, and the effect of righteousness, quietness and assurance forever." Chapter Twelve, Fifteen, Eighteen

Isaiah 40: 29, 31 He gives power to the weak, and to those who have no might He increases strength. But those who wait on the Lord shall renew their strength. Chapter Five

Isaiah 41:10 God said, "Fear not, for I am with you; be not dismayed, for I am your God. I will strengthen you, yes, I will help you, I will uphold you with My righteous right hand." Chapter Five

Isaiah 43:1 But now, thus says the Lord, who created you, O Jacob, and He who formed you, O Israel: "Fear not, for I have redeemed you; I have called you by your name; thou are mine." Chapter Three, Thirteen, Fourteen, Fifteen, Sixteen

Isaiah 43:2, 3 God said, "When you pass through the waters, I will be with you … I am the Lord your God …" Chapter Thirteen, Fourteen, Fifteen, Sixteen

Isaiah 43:4 God said, "Since you were precious in My sight, you have been honored, and I have loved you; therefore I will give men for you, and people for you life." Chapter Four, Eleven, Thirteen, Fourteen, Fifteen, Sixteen

Isaiah 43:5 God said, "Fear not, for I am with you …" Chapter Thirteen, Fourteen, Fifteen, Sixteen

Isaiah 53:4 Of Jesus it was said, "Surely He has borne our griefs and carried our sorrows." Chapter Eight, Sixteen

Isaiah 54:5 For your Maker is your husband, the Lord of hosts is His name; and your Redeemer is the Holy One of Israel; He is called the God of the whole earth. Chapter Sixteen

Isaiah 55:7 God said, "Let the wicked forsake his way, and the unrighteous man his thought. Let him return to the Lord, and He will have mercy on him; and to our God, for He will abundantly pardon." Chapter Eighteen

Isaiah 55:8, 9 "For My thoughts are not your thoughts, neither are your ways My ways," says the Lord. "For as the heavens are higher than the earth, so are My ways higher than your ways, and My thoughts than your thoughts." Chapter Fourteen, Eighteen

Isaiah 57:1 The righteous perishes … the righteous is taken away from evil. Chapter Sixteen

Isaiah 59:2 But your iniquities have separated you from your God… Chapter Nineteen

Isaiah 61:10 I will greatly rejoice in the Lord, my soul shall be joyful in my God; for He has clothed me with the garments of salvation, He has covered me with the robe of righteousness… Chapter Fifteen

James 1:5 If any of you lack wisdom, let him ask of God, who gives to all liberally… Chapter Seven, Fifteen

James 1:17 Every good gift and every perfect gift is from above, and cometh down from the Father of lights, with whom there is no variation, or shadow of turning. Chapter Fourteen, Fifteen

James 5:16 Confess your trespasses to one another, and pray for one another, that you may be healed. The effective, fervent prayer of a righteous man avails much. Chapter Fourteen

Jeremiah 3:14 "Return, O backsliding children," says the Lord; "for I am married to you…" Chapter Sixteen

Jeremiah 29:11 "For I know the thoughts that I think toward you," says the Lord, "thoughts of peace, and not of evil, to give you a future and a hope." Chapter Three, Four, Ten

Jeremiah 31:3 God said, "… I have loved you with an everlasting love; therefore with loving kindness I have drawn you." Chapter Thirteen

I John 1:7 But if we walk in the light as He is in the light, we have fellowship one with another, the blood of Jesus Christ His Son cleanses us from all sin. Chapter Nineteen

I John 1:9 If we confess our sins, He is faithful and just to forgive us our sins and to cleanse us from all unrighteousness. Chapter Nineteen

I John 2:28 And now, little children, abide in Him, that when He shall appear, we may have confidence and not be ashamed before Him at His coming. Chapter Nineteen

I John 3:1 Behold what manner of love the Father has bestowed on us, that we should be called children of God… Chapter Nine

I John 4:4 You are of God, little children, and have overcome them, because He who is in you is greater than he who is in the world. Chapter Three, Seven

John 1:12 But as many as received Him, to them He gave the right to become children of God, even to those who believe in His name. Chapter Eighteen

John 3:16 Jesus said, "For God so loved the world that He gave His only begotten Son, that whoever believes in Him should not perish but have everlasting life." Chapter Three, Fifteen, Nineteen

John 8:32 Jesus said, "And you shall know the truth, and the truth shall make you free." Chapter Five, Twelve, Fourteen, Fifteen

John 8:44 Jesus said, "You are of your father the devil … He was a murderer from the beginning, and does not stand in the truth, because there is no truth in him. When he speaks a lie, he speaks from his own resources, for he is a liar..." Chapter Nine, Twelve, Thirteen, Fifteen, Nineteen

John 10:10 Jcsus said, "The thief does not come except to steal, and to kill, and to destroy. I am come that they may have life, and that they may have it more abundantly." Chapter One, Two, Three, Nine, Thirteen, Fifteen, Sixteen, Nineteen

John 13:35 Jesus said, "By this all will know that you are My disciples, if you have love for one another." Chapter Fourteen

John 14:1-3 Jesus said, "Let not your heart be troubled; you believe in God, believe also in Me. In My Father's house are many mansions; if it were not so, I would have told you. I go to prepare a place for you. And if I go and prepare a place for you, I will come again and receive you to Myself; that where I am, there you may be also." Chapter Nineteen

John 14:6 Jesus said to him, "I am the way, the truth, and the life. No one comes to the Father except through Me." Chapter Twelve, Eighteen

John 14:26 Jesus said, "But the Comforter, which is the Holy Ghost, whom the Father will send in My name, He shall teach you all things, and bring all things to your remembrance, whatsoever I have said unto you." (King James Version of the Bible) Chapter Seventeen

John 14:27 Jesus said, "Peace I leave with you, My peace I give to you; not as the world gives do I give to you. Let not your heart be troubled, neither let it be afraid." Chapter Seventeen

John 15:16 Jesus said, "You did not choose me, but I chose you…" Chapter Thirteen, Eighteen

John 16:12 Jesus said, "I still have many things to say to you, but you cannot bear them now." Chapter Thirteen, Seventeen, Eighteen

John 16:13 Jesus said, "However, when He, the Spirit of truth, has come, He will guide you into all truth..." Chapter Six, Twelve, Thirteen, Fourteen, Seventeen, Eighteen

John 16:20 Jesus said, "Most assuredly, I say to you that you will weep and lament, but the world will rejoice; and you will be sorrowful, but your sorrow will be turned into joy." Chapter Eighteen

John 16:33 Jesus said, "These things I have spoken to you, that in Me you may have peace. In the world you will have tribulation; but be of good cheer, I have overcome the world." Chapter Eighteen

Joshua 24:15 "And if it seems evil to you to serve the Lord, choose for yourselves this day whom you will serve ... but as for me and my house, we will serve the Lord." Chapter Ten

Luke 4:18 Jesus said, "The Spirit of the Lord is upon Me, because He has anointed Me to preach the gospel to the poor. He has sent Me to heal the brokenhearted, to preach deliverance to the captives and recovery of sight to the blind, to set at liberty those who are oppressed." Chapter Twelve, Thirteen, Fourteen, Fifteen, Nineteen

Luke 6:27, 28 Jesus said, "But I say to you who hear: love your enemies, do good to those who hate you. Bless those who curse you, and pray for those who spitefully use you." Chapter Fifteen

Luke **6:36, 38** Jesus said, "Therefore be merciful, just as your Father also is merciful. Give, and it will be given to you: good measure, pressed down, shaken together, and running over will be put into your bosom. For with the same measure that you use, it will be measured back to you." Chapter Sixteen

Luke 23:34 Then said Jesus, "Father, forgive them, for they do not know what they do..." Chapter Fourteen

Malachi 4:6 And He will turn the hearts of the fathers to the children, and hearts of the children to their fathers ... Chapter Fifteen

Mark 10:27 But looking at them, Jesus said, "With men it is impossible, but not with God; for with God all things are possible." Chapter Eighteen

Mark 11:26 Jesus said, "But if you do not forgive, neither will your Father in heaven forgive your trespasses." Chapter Fourteen

Mark 13:13 Jesus said, "And you will be hated of all men for My name's sake. But he who endures to the end shall be saved." Chapter Fifteen

Matthew 1:23 Behold, a virgin shall be with child, and bear a Son, and they shall call His name Immanuel, which is translated, "God with us." Chapter Two, Seventeen, Nineteen

Matthew 4:23, 24 Now Jesus went about all Galilee, teaching in their synagogues, preaching the gospel of the kingdom, and healing all kinds of sickness and all kinds of disease among the people. Then His fame went throughout all Syria; and they brought to Him all sick people who were afflicted with various diseases and torments, and those who were demon-possessed, epileptics, and paralytics; and He healed them. Chapter Thirteen

Matthew 5:5 Jesus said, "Blessed are the meek, for they shall inherit the earth." Chapter Eighteen

Matthew 5:10-12 Jesus said, "Blessed are those who are persecuted for righteousness' sake, for theirs is the kingdom of heaven. Blessed are you when they revile and persecute you, and shall say all kinds of evil against you falsely for My sake. Rejoice and be exceedingly glad, for great is your reward in heaven, for so they persecuted the prophets who were before you." Chapter Eighteen

Matthew 5:44, 45 Jesus said, "But I say unto you, 'Love your enemies, bless those who curse you, do good to those who hate you, and pray for those who spitefully use you and persecute you, that you may be sons of your Father in heaven." Chapter Fifteen

Matthew 6:12 Jesus said, "And forgive us our debts, as we forgive our debtors." Chapter Fourteen

Matthew 6:13 Jesus said, "And do not lead us into temptation, but deliver us from the evil one. For Yours is the kingdom and the power and the glory for ever. Amen." Chapter Two

Matthew 7:12 Jesus said, "Therefore, whatever you want men to do to you, do also to them, for this is the Law and the Prophets." Chapter Sixteen

Matthew 7:21-23 Jesus said, "Not everyone who says to Me, 'Lord, Lord,' shall enter the kingdom of heaven, but he who does the will of My Father in heaven. Many will say to me in that day, 'Lord, Lord, have we not prophesied in Your name, cast out demons in Your name, and done many wonders in Your name?' And then I will declare to them, 'I never knew you; depart from Me, you who practice lawlessness.'" Chapter Nineteen

Matthew 10:21 Jesus said, "Now brother will deliver up brother to death, and a father his child; and children will rise up against parents and cause them to be put to death." Chapter Fifteen

Matthew 11:28-30 Jesus said, "Come to Me, all you who labor and are heavy laden, and I will give you rest. Take My yoke upon you and learn from Me, for I am gentle and lowly in heart, and you will find rest for your souls. For My yoke is easy and My burden is light." Chapter Sixteen, Seventeen

Matthew 13:15, 16 Jesus said, "… lest they should understand with their heart and turn, so that I should heal them. But blessed are your eyes for they see, and your ears for they hear." Chapter Thirteen

Matthew 17:20 Jesus said, "…If ye have faith as a mustard seed, you will say to this mountain, 'Move from here to there'; and it will move; and nothing will be impossible for you." Chapter Thirteen

Matthew 18:6 Jesus said, "But whoever causes one of these little ones who believe in Me to sin, it would be better for him if a millstone were hung around his neck, and he were drowned in the depth of the sea." Chapter One

Matthew chapters 26, 27, 28 Explains the personal trauma, tragedy, and sexual assault Jesus experienced at the end of His life. Chapter Eighteen

Matthew 28:20 Jesus said, "Teaching them to observe all things that I have commanded you; and, lo, I am with you always, even unto the end of the age," Chapter One, Two

Micah 7:6 For son dishonors father, the daughter rises against her mother, daughter-in-law against her mother-in-law; a man's enemies are the men of his own house. Chapter Fifteen

Nahum 1:9 …Affliction will not rise up a second time. Chapter Nineteen

I Peter 3:8, 9 Finally, all of you be of one mind, having compassion for one another. Love as brothers, be tenderhearted, be courteous; not returning evil for evil or reviling for reviling, but on the contrary blessing, knowing that you were called to this, that you may inherit a blessing. Chapter Sixteen, Eighteen

I Peter 5:8 Be sober, be vigilant; because your adversary the devil walks about like a roaring lion, seeking whom he may devour. Chapter Three, Seven

Philippians 1:6 Being confident of this very thing, that He who has begun a good work in you will complete it until the day of Jesus Christ. Chapter Eighteen

Philippians 3:13, 14 …But one thing I do, forgetting those things which are behind and reaching forward to those things which are ahead, I press toward the goal for the prize of the upward call of God in Christ Jesus. Chapter Fourteen, Fifteen, Sixteen, Seventeen

Philippians 4:13 I can do all things through Christ who strengthens me. Chapter Seven, Eighteen

Philippians 4:19 And my God shall supply all your need according to His riches in glory by Christ Jesus. Chapter Seventeen

Psalm 23:1-3 The Lord is my shepherd; I shall not want. He makes me to lie down in green pastures; He leads me beside the still waters. He restores my soul; He leads me in the paths of righteousness for His name's sake. Chapter Eighteen

Psalm 34:1 I will bless the Lord at all times; His praise shall continually be in my mouth. Chapter Twenty

Psalm 34:4, 5 I sought the Lord, and He heard me, and delivered me from all my fears. They looked to Him and were radiant, and their faces were not ashamed. Chapter Twenty

Psalm 34:7, 8 The angel of the Lord encamps all around those that fear Him, and delivers them. Oh, taste and see that the Lord is good; blessed is the man who trusts in Him. Chapter Twenty

Psalm 34:9, 11 Oh, fear the Lord, you His saints! There is no want to those who fear Him. Come, you children, listen to Me; I will teach you the fear of the Lord. Chapter Twenty

Psalm 34:13-14 Keep your tongue from evil, and your lips from speaking guile. Depart from evil, and do good; seek peace, and pursue it. Chapter Twenty

Psalm 34:15 The eyes of the Lord are on the righteous, and His ears are open to their cry. Chapter Eleven, Twenty

Psalm 34:16 The face of the Lord is against those who do evil, to cut off the remembrance of them from the earth. Chapter Twenty

Psalm 34:17, 18 The righteous cry, and the Lord heareth, and delivereth them out of all their troubles. The Lord is nigh unto them that are of a broken heart; and saveth such as be of a contrite Spirit." Chapter Twenty

Psalm 34:19 Many are the afflictions of the righteous; but the Lord delivereth him out of them all. Chapter Twenty

Psalm 34:21 Evil shall slay the wicked, and those who hate the righteous shall be condemned. Chapter Twenty

Psalm 34:22 The Lord redeems the soul of His servants, and none of those who trust in Him shall be condemned. Chapter Twenty

Psalm 40:1, 2 I waited patiently for the Lord; and He inclined to me, and heard my cry. He also brought me up out of a horrible pit, out to the miry clay, and set my feet upon a rock, and established my steps. Chapter Nine, Ten, Fifteen

Psalm 55:22 Cast your burden on the Lord, and He shall sustain you... Chapter Eighteen

Psalm 61:3 For you have been a shelter for me, and a strong tower from the enemy. Chapter Eighteen

Psalm 84:11 For the Lord God is a sun and shield; the Lord will give grace and glory; no good thing will He withhold from those who walk uprightly. Chapter Twenty

Proverbs 1:33 But whoso hearkeneth unto Me shall dwell safely, and shall be quiet from fear of evil. (King James Version) Chapter Four, Eighteen

Proverbs 3:13 Happy is the man who finds wisdom, and the man who gains understanding. Chapter Six

Proverbs 8:13 The fear of the Lord is to hate evil; pride and arrogance and the evil way and the perverse mouth I hate. Chapter Fifteen

Revelation 12:4 His tail drew a third of the stars of heaven and threw them to the earth … Chapter Nineteen

Revelation 12:7, 8 And war broke out in heaven; Michael and His angels fought against the dragon; and the dragon and his angels fought, but they did not prevail, nor was a place found for them in heaven any longer. Chapter Nineteen

Revelation 12:9 So the great dragon was cast out, that serpent of old, called the Devil and Satan, who deceives the whole world; he was cast out to the earth, and his angels were cast out with him. Chapter Nineteen

Revelation 12:10 Then I heard a loud voice saying in heaven, "Now salvation, and strength, and the kingdom of our God, and the power of His Christ have come, for the accuser of our brethren, who accused them before our God day and night, has been cast down." Chapter Eighteen

Revelation 12:12 Therefore rejoice, O heavens, and you who dwell in them! Woe to the inhabitants of the earth and the sea! For the devil has come down to you, having great wrath, because he knows that he has a short time. Chapter Eighteen, Nineteen

Revelation 20:4 …And they lived and reigned with Christ for a thousand years. Chapter Nineteen

Revelation 20:5 But the rest of the dead did not live again until the thousand years were finished. This is the first resurrection. Chapter Nineteen

Revelation 20:10 And the devil, who deceived them, was cast into the lake of fire and brimstone… Chapter Fifteen

Revelation 21:3 And I heard a loud voice from heaven saying, "Behold, the tabernacle of God is with men, and He will dwell with them, and they shall be His people, and God Himself will be with them and be their God." Chapter Nineteen

Revelation 21:4 And God will wipe away every tear from their eyes; there shall be no more death, nor sorrow, nor crying; and there shall be no more pain, for the former things have passed away. Chapter Nineteen

Revelation 21:10 And He carried me away in the Spirit to a great and high mountain, and showed me the great city, the holy Jerusalem, descending out of heaven from God. Chapter Nineteen

Romans 1:29-32 Being filled with all unrighteousness, sexual immorality, wickedness, covetousness, maliciousness; full of envy, murder, strife, deceit, evil-mindedness; they are whisperers, backbiters, haters of God, violent, proud, boasters, inventors of evil things, disobedient to parents, undiscerning, untrustworthy, unloving, unforgiving, unmerciful; who, knowing the righteous judgment of God, that those who practice such things are worthy of death, not only do the same but also approve of those who practice them. Chapter Fifteen

Romans 8:37 Yet in all these things we are more than conquerors through Him who loved us. Chapter Nine, Ten

Romans 12:2 And do not be not conformed to this world, but be transformed by the renewing of your mind, that you may prove what is that good and acceptable and perfect will of God. Chapter Seven, Ten

Romans 12:21 Do not be overcome by evil, but overcome evil with good. Chapter Eighteen

Romans 14:12 So then each of us shall give account of himself to God. Chapter Fifteen

Romans 14:13 Therefore let us not judge one another anymore, but rather resolve this, not to put a stumbling block or a cause to fall in our brother's way. Chapter Fifteen

Romans 15:4 For whatever things were written before were written for our learning, that we through the patience and comfort of the Scriptures might have hope. Chapter Twelve, Thirteen

I Thessalonians 5:9, 10 For God did not appoint us to wrath, but to obtain salvation through our Lord Jesus Christ, who died for us, that whether we wake or sleep, we should live together with Him. Chapter Nineteen

II Timothy 3:15-17 And that from childhood you have known the Holy Scriptures, which are able to make you wise for salvation through faith which is in Christ Jesus. All Scripture is given by inspiration of God, and is profitable for doctrine, for reproof, for correction, for instruction in righteousness, that the man of God may be complete, thoroughly equipped for every good work. Chapter Twelve, Thirteen